KT-234-127

WITHDRAWN FROM
THE LIBRARY

UNIVERSITY OF
WINCHESTER

KA 0394007 1

JITY

This book is a League of Fans project. League of Fans is a sports reform initiative founded by Ralph Nader to encourage civic responsibility in sports industry and culture.

Praise for *How We Can Save Sports*

"Ken Reed's litany of problems and issues besetting American sport—from grassroots to professional levels—is not new. What is new and worthy of a careful read are the author's compelling ideas on what individuals can do about them and why such actions are important. Those with power and a financial self-interest in sport will not be the engineers of reform. Rather, the only hope for a return to 'good' sport will be the activism of those with a moral compass and love of sport who are willing to step forward in their own communities to make change happen one small action at a time."—**Donna Lopiano, president, Sports Management Resources; former CEO, Women's Sports Foundation**

"More than ever in this new gilded age of sports we need Ralph Nader's cold, clear-shooting eye and a game plan for taking back the birthright of athletics. The League of Fans is our best hope."—**Robert Lipsyte, sports journalist, ESPN Ombudsman, and author of *An Accidental Sportswriter***

"Ken Reed's book *How We Can Save Sports* is a reformer's guide to cleaning up sports in America. His prescriptions are worth attention if America is to put sports competition back into perspective. The book takes on the tough questions surrounding the commercialization of sports in America and raises provocative questions about the proper role of sports in our society."—**C. Thomas McMillen, former U.S. congressman; college, NBA, and Olympic athlete**

"*How We Can Save Sports* is an ambitious book with thoughtful responses to virtually every ill facing sports in the United States. Ken Reed has written a valuable book that is both a challenge and a joy. A must read for anyone who cares about what sports could be."—**Jim Thompson, founder & CEO of Positive Coaching Alliance**

"We know that organized sport in America is out of control. Reed's concept of 'citizenship through sports activism' is a much-needed clarion call for all of us to do something about it. More important, he provides a thorough action plan with specific strategies and actions that any citizen who cares deeply about the role of sport in our country can undertake. It's time for all of us to get in the sports reform 'game,' and Reed has provided us with a game plan to do so."—**John R. Gerdy, author of *Ball or Bands: Football vs. Music as an Educational and Community Investment***

"*How We Can Save Sports* is a must read for anyone who wants to right the ship we call SportsWorld, which has so many current crises. I want to share it with all my students in the DeVos Sport Business Management Program."—**Richard Lapchick, chair of DeVos Sport Business Management Program, University of Central Florida**

"According to Ken Reed, sport allows people of all ages to transcend their day-to-day lives in ways that enliven the human spirit. Reed's passionate love of sports informs every page of his book and explains the depth of his criticism of the commercial culture that is corrupting sport from the little league level to the pros. I have never read a book that better explains how commercialism, when out of control, diminishes the joy of sport for fans and participants alike."—**Allen Sack, University of New Haven, author of *Counterfeit Amateurs*; played on Notre Dame's 1966 national championship football team**

"The American sports institution and school-based physical education programs are in crisis. The rising tide of red ink burdening elite collegiate sports programs, the lockouts, strikes, and in some instances, the outright fiscal chaos stalking some professional franchises and leagues, are all hallmarks of current circumstances. Ralph Nader's League of Fans project potentially focuses, escalates, and expands the dialog and debate concerning the core questions at issue here and holds the promise of bringing the broadest spectrum of sports stakeholders into the discussion. On these grounds alone, the League of Fans initiative is not only welcome and needed, it is a national service."—**Harry Edwards, professor emeritus, University of California, Berkeley**

HOW WE CAN SAVE SPORTS

A Game Plan

Ken Reed

Foreword by Ralph Nader

ROWMAN & LITTLEFIELD
Lanham • Boulder • New York • London

UNIVERSITY OF WINCHESTER
LIBRARY

UNIVERSITY OF WINCHESTER

03940071

Published by Rowman & Littlefield
A wholly owned subsidiary of The Rowman & Littlefield Publishing Group, Inc.
4501 Forbes Boulevard, Suite 200, Lanham, Maryland 20706
www.rowman.com

Unit A, Whitacre Mews, 26-34 Stannary Street, London SE11 4AB

Copyright © 2015 by Rowman & Littlefield

All rights reserved. No part of this book may be reproduced in any form or by any
electronic or mechanical means, including information storage and retrieval systems,
without written permission from the publisher, except by a reviewer who may quote
passages in a review.

British Library Cataloguing in Publication Information Available

Library of Congress Cataloging-in-Publication Data Available

ISBN 978-1-4422-4264-7 (cloth : alk. paper)
ISBN 978-1-4422-4265-4 (electronic)

♾™ The paper used in this publication meets the minimum requirements of
American National Standard for Information Sciences—Permanence of Paper
for Printed Library Materials, ANSI/NISO Z39.48-1992.

Printed in the United States of America

To Ralph, the father of the modern consumer movement. Thanks for your belief in the sports project. You are the greatest advocate for the "little guy" of all time.

And to my wife Sandy and daughters Lexi and Angi. I love you three more than anything else in the world. You are—and always will be—the "first" in "first things first."

CONTENTS

FOREWORD

In every known society, no matter its size, anthropologists have found *play* as part of its social fiber. And a major form of play—as a tradition—has been physical sport. Most sport in these early or simpler tribal societies was unorganized where the players outnumbered the spectators (apart from little children). Where sport was organized, as with the Olympics in ancient Athens, the spectators were more numerous than the athletes. But the spectators were allowed to watch for free.

Fast forward to twenty-first-century America. Organized sports—both amateur and professional—have evolved toward ever-superior performance records, rewards, and regalements. This has widened the gap between players and spectators so that the latter regularize themselves as watchers with extensive sports knowledge and a frequent propensity to let sedentary habits increase their weight. For those watchers who are fans in attendance at the arenas and stadiums, their enthusiasms come with stiff ticket, food, and parking prices.

Like most youngsters, I enjoyed sports of the intramural or the sandlot baseball game genre. Lou Gehrig was my hero. The superstar Yankee first baseman's stamina, discipline, and dignity—narrated in books and movies— were inspirational. In those days, major league baseball was king. The NFL and the NBA's precursors were lesser diversions.

The succeeding decades witnessed a massive expansion of sports programming, including endless replaying on cable, and now on smartphones, with a correlative surge of commercialism above everything else. Professional sports are now available to watch 24/7. It is a very serious big business with sales and profits, salaries, corporate luxury suites, and political power burnishing the win-at-all-cost mentalities.

Submerged and subordinated beneath this frenetic rush for money and fame are the traditional physical, mental, and social values of sports for everyone to enjoy, including pursuing happiness and communing with family, neighbors, friends, and coworkers. Our country's allocation of investment in sports entrenches this imbalance between spectator and participatory sports.

Viewing the abuses of the voiceless fans as a consumer protection matter, I, together with Peter Gruenstein, started a nonprofit group called FANS in the late 1970s. Peter's monthly newsletter became a focal point for tight reporting on the mistreatment of fans, taxpayers, and communities by commercial sports leagues. Howard Cosell referred to FANS on *Monday Night Football*. But for a variety of reasons—including lack of resources and Peter going to Alaska to write a book about that state—FANS suspended operations.

Now comes the recharged League of Fans and this sports manifesto, written by our sports policy director, Ken Reed. Immersed in sports as a player, coach, marketer, teacher, and writer, Dr. Reed shares our belief that much that is wrong in sports—at all levels—has been exposed but little has been advocated, much less remedied. As usual, the reason is that fans and sports participants, as citizens, are not organized to move their grievances and broader values into a reform drive. In *How We Can Save Sports*, Reed wants to connect both with fans' and participants' best instincts and sense of fair play, and with anyone else in the sportsphere—active or retired—who wishes to pursue these common causes.

I hope the constituencies for each subject in this book who want wider public debate and action will find further support behind their elevated purposes for sports. They have labored long and hard—some of their work is included in this book—and deserve more recognition and support. They are parents, coaches, players or former players, academics, educators, physicians, reporters, authors, and civil rights advocates, who have scored some victories for change, but who remain frustrated at the slow pace of necessary transformation.

Finally, a reflection here on the sports media is pertinent. While some members of this sprightly styled profession occasionally pause from their horserace duties to highlight some fairly unsafe, crude, and greedy aspects of sports, by and large the ample daily pages, radio/TV stations, and bloggers cover spectator sports in a routine fashion and ignore other aspects of the sports world altogether, including sports activities and issues at the community level. I've often wondered why the sports pages do not fairly title their section "Spectator Sports" to better describe their craft.

To make any changes or reforms—or to even take wholly fresh looks at sport in all its exciting dimensions—the fans and the media need each other. Without the media widening its space for the civic activity on these issues and other topics, editors and reporters might ask themselves what the ultimate purpose is for their occasional exposés or grounded criticisms of professional sports as usual—or college, high school, and youth sports for that matter.

The culture of sports invites a fresh spring of renewal and wider embrace.

Ralph Nader, Washington D.C.

PREFACE

Sport deserves a more critical examination.
We need to ask more probing questions about sport.

Rick Reilly, sportswriter and author

I love sports.

I'm also fed up with sports.

I'm guessing that if you have any interest in what this book is all about you're conflicted in the same way.

I've been involved in the world of sports, in one capacity or another, my entire life. Born the son of a coach, I played organized competitive athletics from Little League through college. I've been a coach at multiple levels, a scout, a sports administrator, a sports marketing consultant, a sports studies professor, and a sports issues columnist.

It's safe to say that sports have influenced who I am today—for better or worse—more than anything else. It's the single thread woven throughout my life experience.

I have a heartfelt passion for sports, although many people, including a few family members and several friends, think I'm actually anti-sports—or at least way too negative about sports. They say I spend too much time talking and writing about the problems, issues, and challenges in SportsWorld and not enough time focusing on the good things.

On several occasions, people have asked me, "Why are you so angry about all these sports issues?"

My response is always, "Why aren't *you* angry?"

Robert F. Kennedy once said, "The sharpest criticism often goes hand in hand with the deepest idealism and love of country."

I think that sentiment holds true for sports as well. I believe those who truly love sports should continually work to improve the sports experience for everyone involved. Collectively and individually, we should strive to enhance the positives and mitigate the negatives for all sports stakeholders.

That's what I'm about. And that's what this book is about.

There are indeed many good things about sports. Sport is a sociocultural institution of much value for a society's citizens. However, it shouldn't be driven by win-at-all-costs (WAAC) and profit-at-all-costs (PAAC) values from the professional level all the way down to the youth level. There are fundamental social justice issues in sports today that simply aren't being addressed seriously enough.

And it's up to us—those who love sports—to do it.

As the sports sociologist Jay Coakley wrote in his seminal book *Sports in Society: Issues and Controversies*, "Unless we work to create the sports we want in the future, sports will represent the interests of those who want us to play on their terms and for their purposes. This leaves us with an interesting choice: we can be consumers who accept sports as they are, or we can be citizens who use sports as contexts for actively making the world a better place."

In effect, what I'm promoting in this book is "citizenship through sports activism." I want to help inspire thousands of potential sports activists and reformers across the United States to work toward a more evenhanded sports experience in America.

We can't count on Big Sport (primarily professional sports and highly commercialized college sports) organizations and individuals to spur change in a system that provides them with numerous economic and political advantages. Change must come from the grassroots, through sports citizens and their individual and collective activism and reform initiatives.

Together we need to promote fairer sports policies and push our sports organizations to be more socially responsible in their decision making and actions.

The syndicated columnist Molly Ivins once said her driving purpose was to answer the questions, "Who's getting screwed?" and "Who's doing the screwing?" I want to do that too, relative to SportsWorld. But I want to move beyond that to promoting a few potential solutions to many of the problems in our sports culture today.

I consider this book a sports manifesto. According to *Webster's*, a manifesto is a public declaration of intentions, motives, or views. That's a pretty good description of what this book is all about, in terms of the key issues impacting sports fans, athletes, consumers, and taxpayers.

It's time to get started. But first we need a quick overview of where we're at and how we got here.

1

OUR SPORTS HAVE BEEN SEIZED BY THE FORCES OF EGO AND GREED

We're witnessing the takeover of one of our most cherished cultural practices, sport. In effect, owners and other sports power brokers with win-at-all-costs (WAAC) and profit-at-all-costs (PAAC) agendas are hijacking the joy of sports. Our sports belong to us. They came up from the people. They were invented for reasons having nothing to do with money or ego. We can't sit still while greedy individuals, corporations, and other power brokers take them from us for their own purposes.

Ralph Nader, founder, League of Fans

Too often, when developing sports policies in this country, the first questions asked by those in power—team owners, executives, league commissioners, college sports administrators, and other sports managers—are usually some form of "What's in it for me/us?" and/or "How can I/we make more money off this game and the people who love it?" Instead of "What's best for the game?" "What's best for the players?" and "What's best for the fans?"

The commercialization and professionalization abuses addressed in this book—from the professional level down to the youth level—are the result of the current overriding drivers of American sport policy: ego and greed. This typically manifests itself in the form of an insatiable, and often unethical, lust for winning, money, or both—no matter the consequences for the game or the people involved.

In effect, sports in America are suffering from soul sickness. Too often, our sports aren't what they can be at their best. The number of ethical and sociocultural issues and challenges in the world of sports has never been greater. Consider the following brief sample:

- Wide-ranging academic corruption in college and high school athletic programs.
- The college sports cartel (Big Ten, Big 12, Pac-12, Atlantic Coast Conference, Southeastern Conference) that runs big-time college football in the Football Bowl Subdivision (FBS)—formerly known as NCAA Division I—limits opportunities (i.e., a fair shot at a national championship) for the conferences and schools left on the outside of their cartel. (This has historically been done through the Bowl Championship Series [BCS] system and its predecessors. Starting in 2014, it is done through an access-limiting four-team play-off.)
- The perversity known as PSLs, in which pro and college football teams force loyal fans to purchase personal seat licenses (PSLs) just to have the *right* to buy season tickets.
- NFL franchises requiring season ticket holders to purchase preseason (read: exhibition) game tickets at full regular season prices.
- Publicly financed stadiums, arenas, and sweetheart leases for wealthy owners who have the capacity to build privately financed stadiums and arenas.
- Incessant work stoppages in the professional sports leagues in which fans have no voice.
- Exorbitant ticket and concession prices at taxpayer-funded stadiums (at which most, if not all, ticket, concession, merchandise, and parking revenues typically go directly to the franchise owners via sweetheart leases).
- Television blackouts originating from taxpayer-financed stadiums, which means the local citizens that built the stadiums can't watch games from their own stadiums.
- Excessive and increasing commercialization in our little leagues and high schools.
- A focus on varsity athletic teams for elite athletes in high schools and middle schools, while intramural sports programs and physical education classes for all students gradually go the way of the dinosaur.
- College athletes having to pay all, or part, of their own medical bills, even though they were injured while playing for their university.
- Disparities in opportunities for females, disabled individuals, and people of color in our schools despite Title IX and other civil rights advances.

- The proliferation of youth club sports organizations that, in reality, have a financial versus an educational and child development mission.
- The specialization and professionalization of young athletes at earlier and earlier ages, resulting in the "burnout" phenomenon and a rise in overuse injuries.
- The increasing use of performance-enhancing drugs (PEDs) at all ages, by both males and females.
- The erosion of the core ideals, values, and ethics of sports, resulting in escalating incidents of poor sportsmanship.
- An increase in sports injuries across all levels, most alarmingly concussions and other brain trauma injuries.
- A failure to properly and effectively address the concussion issue by sports organizations at all levels.
- A shocking increase in physical inactivity and obesity in the United States, especially among our young people.
- The prevalence of dehumanizing coaches at all levels, most disturbingly at the youth level.
- A sports media that does a good job reporting scores, developing sports personality features, and addressing personnel issues (e.g., who should Team X trade, draft, or recruit) but, for the most part, drops the ball on the important social, cultural, and economic issues in sports.

The list goes on and on.

WAAC AND PAAC: THE FUNDAMENTAL CAUSES OF VIRTUALLY ALL PROBLEMS IN SPORTS

Sports are a great thing when the influences of ego and greed are minimized. The problems start when ego and greed begin to drive the sports policy-and-decision-making bus.

When the desires to win and make money at all costs are the only, or even primary, motivators in sport—completely neglecting human considerations and what's best for the sport as a whole—sport begins to lose its way, at all levels.

As such, our overarching challenge as people who care about sports and the people involved in them is to confront and overcome the WAAC and PAAC mentalities, policies, and decisions that are resulting in a variety of abuses in SportsWorld—from the pros down to our little leagues.

In today's SportsWorld, WAAC and PAAC philosophies and actions are negatively impacting sports fans, participants, taxpayers, and other stakeholders, as well as threatening the integrity and essence of sport—its ideals, values, principles, ethics, and traditions.

The cornerstone of virtually every issue and problem in the world of sports today can be traced back to WAAC and PAAC mentalities and policies.

Striving to win isn't the problem. That's part of the essence of sport. Striving to win at all costs is the problem.

Similarly, striving to make a profit in the sports business isn't the problem. Striving to make a profit at all costs—above all other values—is the problem.

WAAC and PAAC values distort the original reasons for sport: play, exercise, socialization, community bonding, education, health and wellness, fun, a form of individual expression, competition as a means of bringing out the best in all participants, etc.

"Sport is consistently appropriated by commercial interests and we've lost control of the playing conditions," says sports sociologist Jay Coakley. "Sports have moved to emphasizing the spectacle aspect of sports in order to cater to spectators. These characteristics have worked against sports on their own terms."

Let's be clear, commercialization in sport isn't all bad. Commercialization has, in many cases, created opportunities for athletes that otherwise wouldn't have been there. Little League baseball teams have long been sponsored by community businesses. Without these sponsorships, opportunities for young baseball players would have been limited, and even out of the reach of some families. In addition, commercialization has fueled professional leagues that have given amateur athletes, including women, opportunities to continue playing sport at a high level after their college eligibility has expired.

Moreover, there are many instances where enjoyment levels for spectators have been enhanced by commercialization. For example, the traditional company-sponsored "jersey nights" around major league and minor league ballparks. For decades, kids have been filled with joy when they're handed a team jersey—albeit one with a corporate logo plastered on it—as they walk through the stadium gates.

WAAC AND PAAC CONSIDERATIONS IN PROFESSIONAL SPORTS

It's important to note that athletes and fans have a passion for sports that is unmatched by consumers in other industries, with the possible exception of the music industry. For example, consider the famous "Deadheads" who have followed the Grateful Dead around the country through the years, or Bruce Springsteen's passionate legion of supporters the past several decades.

Despite how many sports executives behave, sport isn't just an industry, it's a sociocultural institution. Therefore, due to sociocultural reasons, sport as business is different than any other business, and needs to be treated as such.

Fans of sports teams—whether professional or college—emotionally identify with team colors, names, uniforms, logos, traditions, etc., in a way that never happens in other industries. It becomes part of their personal identity. Thus, when franchise owners, marketers, and corporate sponsors trample on these types of things, with almost total disregard for the tradition, history, and values of sports in general and/or the team in particular, fans feel alienated and angry.

If you want to see people riled up, try taking the pinstripes off the New York Yankees home uniforms or moving the Boston Red Sox out of Fenway Park. You'll have hell to pay. Chicago Cubs fans started screaming when word got out that the Cubs' ownership wanted to "modernize" venerable Wrigley Field by doing things like putting up video boards around the ballpark.

People simply have much stronger feelings for franchises like the Yankees, Red Sox, and Cubs than they do for companies in other industries, for instance IBM. There's an emotional, almost spiritual, attachment to the Yankees. Even fans of the team's archrival, the Red Sox, would be upset if Yankees owners removed the pinstripes from the Yankees home uniforms.

The Yankee pinstripes are part of the Yankees–Red Sox rivalry and part of baseball lore and tradition. They are an aspect of the overall appeal of the game, no matter who your favorite team is. People don't like sports tradition messed with.

That's why there's always an uproar from fans when the possibility of corporate logos on uniforms comes up. Can you imagine the iconic Los Angeles Lakers uniforms with McDonald's golden arches sewn on?

When a nonsports corporation leaves a city, there can be some gnashing of teeth for economic reasons but there is usually very little emotional or spiritual attachment to the departing business on the part of the citizens of the community. On the other hand, cities and fans "adopt" pro franchises as their own. That's unique among all industries. More than half a century later, there is still a lot of anger in Brooklyn—and elsewhere, for that matter—over the Dodgers' ugly departure for Los Angeles.

Professional sports are increasingly a grotesque distortion of what they could be at their best. We're moving steadily toward overt commercial spectacle, and away from sports; closer to mixed martial arts (MMA) than pure athletic competition. Scantily clad "cheerleaders," obnoxious mascots, nonstop blaring loudspeakers, flashing scoreboards, and commercial messages everywhere one looks in a stadium or arena make the athletic competition just one aspect of the overall commercialized spectacle today.

When sport is driven solely by commercial and entertainment ethics you end up with something like the absurdity known as the XFL, a caricature of the sport of football. The XFL played one season, in 2001. It was a combination of professional football and the spectacle that is professional wrestling.

The XFL model was football chaos, with fewer rules than the NFL, trash-talking public address announcers, etc. Football's values and traditions were a complete afterthought. The entire league was driven by entertainment and marketing sensibilities. It basically failed due to the nonexistence of sport ethos in the operation of its league.

There's a lesson in the XFL's demise for all professional sport leagues and big-time college sports programs: Tread carefully in your ongoing march toward the XFL model of crass entertainment and commercialism.

WAAC AND PAAC CONSIDERATIONS IN COLLEGE SPORTS

In the early days of college athletics, students organized and coached their own teams. Today athletic departments have become stand-alone business empires at many Division I campuses. In effect, they are autonomous, for-profit entities operating under the guise of the university's nonprofit umbrella. Presidents have surrendered their oversight responsibilities, pressured by alums and boosters who want to see their university win games.

The sad Penn State scandal is an extreme, but telling, example of what can happen when there's a complete loss of institutional control of the athletics department on the part of presidents and boards of trustees.

The academic qualifications of recruited athletes become a secondary consideration for the vast majority of big-time college programs. The goal is simply to get superior athletes into school—and keep them eligible—at all costs. In fact, at many schools, athletes are accepted on a "special admit" basis that allows them to enter without having to meet normal entrance requirements. In some cases, the university president personally signs off on these special admits. This type of special admits policy is active even in the Ivy League, which has long promoted its "we have sports in perspective" image.

To win, and to fill humongous stadiums and arenas, elite athletes must be recruited. To that end, plush "athletic centers" with massive weight rooms, locker rooms, study centers, and other facilities are constructed as marketing tools to lure these athletes.

In recent years, many college athletic departments have surrendered a lot of control to corporate sponsors. Companies like Nike and Under Armour exert control in so many areas today that one could argue they are de facto co-athletic directors at big-time sports universities. They influence uniform design, colors, coaches' compensation, marketing strategies, etc. In some cases, Nike has developed a clause in its contract with universities that bars any employee of the school from speaking negatively about the company sponsoring athletics. The schools have agreed. A strange capitulation for these bastions of academic freedom, wouldn't you say?

One of the side effects of the WAAC and PAAC mentalities running rampant on our college campuses is the exploitation of the athletes. College athletes at big-time NCAA Division I programs are in effect both students and athletes—not "student-athletes," as the NCAA proclaims in an effort to protect the myth of amateurism. The reality is these athletes don't enjoy the same basic economic and civil rights as other students on campus.

Civil rights historian Taylor Branch says the civil rights issue of our time is college athletes being prohibited from being fairly compensated in the marketplace under the guise of amateurism.

"The governance of college sports is a civil rights issue because the athletes are citizens and are being denied their rights by what amounts to collusion," says Branch. "Colleges are telling football and basketball players they can't get anything above a college scholarship. The athletes are being conned out of their rights. We need modern abolitionists to fight this unjust and unstable system."

WAAC AND PAAC CONSIDERATIONS IN HIGH SCHOOL AND YOUTH SPORTS

Despite what we're witnessing in professional and big-time college sports, the most insidious effect of WAAC and PAAC thinking is the impact this approach has on the lower levels of sports in this country. There is a strong connection between how sports are operated at the professional and big-time college levels and what's happening at the high school, youth, and community sports levels.

In a nation with very little in the way of actual public policy in the sports realm, what we're left with is sports policy being set by executives at the highest level of sports—professional and big-time college sports—which then trickles down. And what trickles down is rarely in the best interests of the stakeholders at the lower levels.

Increasingly, educational, physical, emotional, and spiritual developmental goals for college, high school, and youth sports programs are being brushed aside by Big Sport's win-at-all-costs and profit-at-all-costs ethos.

The professionalization of youth sports organizations, our "little leagues," is especially appalling. Adults—parents and coaches—are treating youth sports like the big-time pro and college versions. Kids quickly learn from the adults in their lives that winning is priority one, whether that ethic is verbalized or not.

It doesn't have to be that way, and it shouldn't, says Diana Cutaia, former longtime athletic director at Wheelock College and currently a sports consultant who spends a lot of her time fighting WAAC mentalities from the youth level to the college level.

"My evaluation model is not based on wins and losses," said Cutaia, while Wheelock's athletic director. "I evaluate on a variety of other things—each of which could potentially impact the win-loss record in positive ways. We strive to win but winning games and championships isn't why our athletic department exists. It is interesting to note, however, that when we started measuring success in other ways besides wins and losses, we started seeing more wins."

Sadly, the professionalization of youth sports has resulted in virtually total control by adults today. Spontaneous play, where kids form teams, make up the rules, and design their own plays has been replaced by adult-controlled youth sports, in which "grown-ups" create the leagues, teams, make the rules, design and call the plays—often for their own entertainment and ego gratification and, even worse, sometimes simply to realize a profit.

It's not uncommon for youth football teams, made up of ten- and eleven-year-olds, to have six coaches, including offensive and defensive coordinators. Young people become nothing more than performers in a youth sports entertainment spectacle, under the authoritarian oversight of the head coach.

Veteran sports journalist Robert Lipsyte describes the all too common youth sports environment this way: "A million Little Leaguers stand for hours while a criminally obese "coach" drills the joy of sport out of their souls, makes them self-conscious and fearful, teaches them technique over movement, emphasizes dedication, sacrifice, and obedience instead of accomplishment and fun."

Specialization is another trend in the movement to professionalize our young athletes. Athletes are specializing in a single sport at younger and younger ages. Many ten- to twelve-year-old soccer, volleyball, basketball, baseball, and softball players are pressured by parents and coaches to play competitively in one sport, year-round, in an effort to maximize the young athlete's development. This, despite quantitative and qualitative research that has shown that early specialization in one sport is rarely beneficial, and is often detrimental, to an athlete's overall development. Moreover, research also reveals that kids who specialize in one sport at an early age burn out sooner and suffer more from overuse injuries. Nevertheless, parents are increasingly shipping their kids to specialized sports trainers for training regimens similar to what major college and pro athletes go through.

As the perceived rewards become greater (athletic scholarships, professional sports contracts, Olympic team berths, etc.), parents are putting more and more time and money into youth sports. Many families, most often middle- and upper-middle-class suburbanites, will have spent tens of thousands of dollars on club teams, personal training, travel leagues, etc., by the time their child is a senior in high school, all in the hopes of landing a major college athletic scholarship—an occurrence that is much more rare than most parents and their children realize.

A disturbing trend at the high school level is the increasing infiltration of corporations onto high school campuses. High schools around the country are now known as "Coke schools" or "Pepsi schools." These high schools, in search of revenue to support dwindling sports budgets—or simply to keep up with the Joneses—have turned to corporate sponsors to fill the bill. Stadiums, gyms, locker rooms, and other facilities are now plastered with corporate brands, often "junk food" companies eager to exploit an easily susceptible target audience. All of this while the country is in the middle of a childhood obesity epidemic.

Where has this win-at-all-costs and profit-at-all-costs model of youth sports led us? Studies have shown that one-third of all kids in sports drop out each year, and 80 percent drop out of sports completely between ages twelve and sixteen.

The bottom line is we're using a youth sports model that's failing to build a lifetime love of sport and physical fitness.

CHANGING OUR SPORTS CULTURE

Clearly, from a sports policy perspective, what we're currently doing as a country isn't fully beneficial to key sports stakeholders at the pro, college, high school, or youth levels.

However, is change even possible?

Sports sociologist D. Stanley Eitzen did a nice job answering that question when he wrote the following in his book *Fair and Foul*: "Sport, as it is practiced in the United States, is not fated by nature or even by the 'invisible hand' of the market; it is a social construction, the result of historical actions and choices. Americans have created the organization of sport that now exists, and Americans maintain it. This means, then, that because sport is created by people, it can be changed by them as well."

Sports have always had an incredible potential for representing the diversity and positive qualities of American culture while overcoming injustice, intolerance, and stereotypes. But the sports industry often suppresses this potential and avoids many of the societal problems that it has helped to create.

The benefits to society that sports can provide, and the life lessons they can teach our youth, are undeniable. But the excesses of the sports industry have taken control of the games and undermined the benefits. Too often today sport reflects an ethos that is entirely different from traditional sports values, and it primarily revolves around money: e.g., marketing, commercialism, exploitation of America's youth, and greed.

To save sports in this country, we need sports leaders and policy makers who fully incorporate social and cultural considerations—not just economic considerations—in their decision making. We need sports policies that put people, and what's best for the games themselves, first—ahead of winning and money.

Philosopher and conservative political writer Michael Novak eloquently described the challenge this way:

> Sports are not merely entertainment, but are rooted in the necessities and the aspirations of the human spirit. They should be treated with all the intelligence, care, and love the human spirit can bring to bear. It is a corruption, not only of sports, but also of the human spirit, to treat them as escape, entertainment, business, or a means of making money. Sports *do* provide entertainment, but of a special and profound sort. They *do* depend upon a financial base, and it is not wrong that they should repay investors and players decent returns. Yet sports are at their heart a spiritual activity, a natural religion, a tribute to grace, beauty, and excellence. We ought to keep the streams of the spirit running clean and strong.

Indeed, sport can be beautiful when WAAC and PAAC mentalities are absent and ugly when they are present.

In effect, the challenge we're looking at is truly a fight for the soul of sports. It will take passion, determination, and perseverance to take back our sports. Fortunately, history provides examples to guide and inspire us.

Sports have been changed for the better due to the concerted efforts of both individuals and groups. Historically, these sports activists and reformers—often exhibiting great courage—were part of underlying social movements that fought—and changed—the status quo.

It's never easy. And it's usually not quick. Sports reform is often a marathon, not a sprint. But change *does* happen.

Consider three well-known examples:

Jackie Robinson and Branch Rickey Lead the Integration of Baseball

As most everyone is well aware, Major League Baseball was segregated for a lengthy part of its history. Our "national" pastime basically hung out a sign that read "For Whites Only." If you had asked a hundred people associated with baseball before World War II if the Major Leagues would ever integrate, the vast majority of them would've said "No way."

But in 1947 Brooklyn Dodgers owner and executive Branch Rickey brought Jackie Robinson into the major leagues against the heavy opposition of almost everyone associated with the game. In fact, Major League owners voted against Rickey's proposal to integrate baseball by a fifteen to one margin in 1946. At the time, a vote among the players would've resulted in a similar landslide statement against integration.

Nevertheless, Rickey and Robinson prevailed and sparked integration in the major leagues. Within a decade, many African American ballplayers became stars and would eventually be accepted—and in some cases adored—by players and fans of all colors.

But it wasn't Rickey and Robinson alone. There were other activists, with lower profiles, who helped with baseball's integration. Newspaper writers like Lester Rodney pointed out that while African Americans fought in World War II to help protect our freedoms, American society still denied them the opportunity to compete on the playing field with whites in Major League Baseball.

A handful of others inside baseball, including the new, more open-minded, commissioner Happy Chandler—who succeeded segregationist Kenesaw Mountain Landis—quietly helped in the desegregation movement in a less visible way than that of Rickey and Robinson.

Baseball Players Win the Right to Free Agency

Until the mid-1970s, Major League Baseball players were trapped on one team by the reserve clause in their contracts. Unlike the rest of us, they couldn't choose their employer. Once a player signed with a particular team, the franchise had the rights to that player for life. The player couldn't negotiate with another team. The only way a player could move to another team was to be cut, sold, or traded. If a team owner decided to sell or trade player X to a team in another city, it was "tough luck" for the player. Player X had no input in the matter. His options were to pick up his family and move, or quit.

The reserve clause was designed by owners to keep player salaries artificially low and restrict basic freedoms the rest of Americans enjoyed. Because owners had been granted an antitrust exemption by the government, they could pretty much do what they wanted. It was the closest thing to owning a plantation since the Civil War ended slavery in America.

Eventually, the baseball players' union, the Major League Players Association, became collectively stronger under union head Marvin Miller. The union began to push back against the reserve clause. Then a courageous player named Curt Flood brought a suit against baseball and its reserve clause after the St. Louis Cardinals traded him to the Philadelphia Phillies following the 1969 season. Flood refused to go, sitting out the 1970 season. The case went all the way to the U.S. Supreme Court where Flood lost five to three. However, the court made note that the system should be changed by congressional action. It never was. Nevertheless, Flood had sparked the engine of change.

After Flood's Supreme Court case, momentum for ending the reserve clause continued to grow. In the early 1970s, arbitrators released three Major League Baseball players from their teams in contract disputes revolving around the legality of the reserve clause. These players ended up signing with other teams for salaries much greater than what they had been paid by their previous teams. Ultimately, the owners reached an agreement with the players' union on the reserve clause, opening up the free agency era. Miller, Flood, Andy Messersmith, and a few other strong-willed ballplayers had led the way to dramatic change.

Miller's efforts on behalf of the players during his time as head of the players' union resulted in many positive changes in Major League Baseball. In fact, Miller has a strong résumé for induction into the Baseball Hall of Fame. Unfortunately, he is still on the outside of the Hall looking in. This is a major oversight. As baseball great Reggie Jackson once said, "Miller had more influence on Major League Baseball than anyone ever."

Title IX and Gender Equity

Title IX had its genesis when a small faction of the National Organization of Women (NOW) gathered data on discrimination against women in community and school sports. Armed with this information, and eventually joined by hundreds of other sports activists, NOW began lobbying Congress for equal treatment. Ultimately, Congress passed Title IX, which requires schools that receive federal funds to provide equal opportunities for males and females, including, but certainly not limited to, athletics.

Until Title IX was enacted in 1972, girls and women with an interest in sports were basically told to take a seat in the stands or grab a pom-pom. Sports were the special province of boys and men.

As a result of the opportunities created by Title IX, more than three million girls play sports in high school today compared to fewer than three hundred thousand before Title IX.

The NCAA initially fought Title IX but eventually turned completely around on the issue as grassroots-based political pressure increased.

"Athletics participation is of value to both men and women. Let us leave no one behind because we think sport participation is the right of one gender over another," said former NCAA president Myles Brand.

The tremendous success of Title IX can be traced to a small group of passionate activists that grew into a powerful reform movement, one that not only created opportunities and improved conditions for females in the world of sports but also, indirectly, had a positive impact in the workplace and other areas of society.

THE CHALLENGE FOR ALL OF US WHO LOVE SPORTS

Unlike numerous countries that have government-sponsored sports policy organizations, and/or "ministers of sport," to lead sports policy development from the youth and recreational levels to the Olympic and professional levels, sports policy development and implementation in the United States is primarily carried out by the leagues, associations, and commissions that have a vested economic interest in the outcome.

That's the foundation of the core problem we face in the sports-reform movement: Sports policy in America is driven almost exclusively by economic considerations. In the United States, the "caretakers" of sport are also the barons of sport, those with a commercial stake.

At some point, you would think these caretakers of sports in the United States would say, "Not everything in sports is for sale." However, that doesn't seem to be the case. Seldom are the needs, wants, hopes, and expectations of all sports stakeholders considered by those who make economic considerations their number one priority when making sports policy decisions.

The corporations and powerful executives who control sport—and are advantaged by the status quo—will be reluctant to make even minor changes on their own accord. Moreover, Big Sport will resist any significant reform efforts coming from the outside.

Nevertheless, the effort must be made. Sport is an important aspect of our society. As author and public policy consultant Varda Burstyn says, "The rituals of sport engage more people in a shared experience than any other institution or cultural activity today."

It's important that the individuals and organizations that have the power to shape sports policy in the United States act in a socially responsible way. To that end, checks and balances are needed. That's where all of us who love sports come in.

It's time for us to individually and collectively work to stem the tide on the WAAC and PAAC abuses that are negatively impacting our sports. We need to reestablish the original ideals and values of sports. We can no longer afford to stand idly by and surrender sports to those looking to use them as just another way to make big bucks.

Whatever our role in sports—from participant to fan to sports consumer to good old-fashioned taxpayer—we can't allow those with PAAC and WAAC agendas to establish the policies that will determine how we, the people, experience *our* sports—from the professional level down to the youth level.

If we truly care about sports—and *all* the stakeholders involved—we need to be sports reformers and sports activists in our own way—even if that means just pushing for a policy change at the local Little League board meeting.

We owe it to ourselves, and our children, to become informed citizens and sports activists who try to make the world a better place through sports. And we owe it to all the sports activists and reformers who've come before us—those who made sports more fair, just, and ethical in their day.

"The popular stereotype of today's sports reformer is that of a person who doesn't like athletes or sports competition and would like to see youth, scholastic, amateur, and collegiate sports greatly reduced or eliminated," says sports reformer Bruce Svare. "Not only is this stereotype inaccurate, but it is the exact opposite of what most sports reformers are like today. Many of those in the sports reform field are former athletes, coaches, and athletic administrators. They have a strong appreciation for what it takes to be top athletes and to succeed academically. Their dedication to sports and their desire to end exploitation and abuse of athletes motivates them to seek change. Indeed, it can be said that the most stable, loyal, and empathetic friend of the athlete is the sports reformer."

Those of us who love sports didn't *choose* to fall in love with sports. At some point it just happened. However, many of us feel like we're falling out of love with sports these days. Too often we feel the egos in sports have run amok and the whole greedy mess has gotten too ugly. But deep down inside each of us, there's a place that believes if sports were done right (more fairly, justly, equitably, and ethically)—minus the ego and greed—we could love them again.

If that resonates with you, there's a path you can take. You can become a sports reformer, an activist in your own way. It doesn't require quitting your job or ignoring your family. And you can be a passionate reformer without becoming jaded about sports. It simply means doing what you can in your sphere to make the world of sports better from this day forward.

But it will require an active choice on your part. While we didn't *choose* when or how we fell in love with sports, we do need to *choose* to become sports reformers and work toward enhancing the positives and eliminating the negatives in sports.

You'll find plenty of ideas in this book. But some of the best sports-reform outcomes have resulted from efforts driven by personal passion.

"By promoting reforms in countless community, state, regional and national sports organizations, average citizens can be the instruments for change," says Svare. "All causes require this kind of grassroots effort, and sports reform is no different. The alternative—inaction and continued apathy—will only hasten the growth of a negative sports system that is devouring everything in its path."

If you love something, you'll fight to protect it, you'll do what's needed to save and preserve it. Do a little reflection. What can *you* do to help improve the world of sports in your community, state, or nation?

As activist sports journalist Dave Zirin says, "There's a time to cheer and a time to seethe. We all have a stake in knowing the difference."

2

TRANSITION TO COMMUNITY OWNERSHIP MODEL WOULD EMPOWER FANS

The self-regulated monopoly system in pro sports—including anti-trust exemptions—has allowed owners to pursue a profit-at-all-costs agenda at the expense of fans. This system has resulted in owners playing one city off another in the quest for new taxpayer-funded stadiums and other freeloading. A community ownership model, like the Green Bay Packers', works. It's a better way to structure and administer professional sports. It should become an optional mainstay of sports policy in this country. Yet, more Green Bay models are explicitly prohibited by the NFL.

Ralph Nader, founder, League of Fans

In the United States, we socialize the debt of sports and privatize the profits.

Dave Zirin, sports journalist

The fundamental problem in professional sports is that each sport is a self-regulated monopoly. Our pro sports leagues—and the franchise owners within—have basically been given free rein in the United States.

As a result, our old friends' egos and greed are driving policy making and decision making in professional sports. A profit-at-all-costs (PAAC) mentality is at the root of virtually every action taken by pro sports owners. And a win-at-all-costs (WAAC) philosophy supports that PAAC mentality. The results are seldom pretty.

UNIVERSITY OF WINCHESTER LIBRARY

Owners are unencumbered when it comes to their cartel practices. They do not have to deal with the checks and balances of an open marketplace *or* the oversight of public regulation agencies like other monopolistic industries in the United States.

It's a system that needs changing.

A quick story that provides a feel for the issue: The Denver Broncos had just won the Super Bowl in 1998. *Sporting News* had named Denver as the top-rated sports town in the country. The Broncos had sold out every home game at Mile High Stadium for well over a decade. Nevertheless, Broncos' owner Pat Bowlen threatened to take his Broncos out of town unless Denver came up with $250 million for a new stadium. The team was only estimated to be worth $180 million at the time. As is often the case, the city (read: its taxpayers) came up with the dough. The Broncos stayed.

Now that's a rotten system for everyone but franchise owners. It's a system that allows franchise blackmail or, as some owners have called it, with a wink of the eye, "franchise free agency."

THE SPORTS TAX

Pro sports franchise owners and big-time college sports administrators have long been masters at getting taxpayers to pay for a big chunk of their expenses. The most obvious example is publicly funded stadiums and arenas for wealthy NFL, NBA, MLB, and NHL franchise owners. These owners have regularly teamed with local politicians to create schemes in which local taxpayers end up paying for sports palaces so rich owners can get richer.

However, professional sports franchise owners enjoy many other financial benefits because of favorable tax treatment.

Political columnist David Sirota uses the term "Sports Tax" as a catch-all label for key levies the "little guy" is being forced to pay. Sirota identifies four aspects of the Sports Tax. The first one is direct handouts. Sirota cites a *Bloomberg Businessweek* report that reveals "taxpayers have committed $18.6 billion since 1992 to subsidies for the NFL's 32 teams, counting the expense of building stadiums, forgone real estate taxes, land and infrastructure improvements, and interest costs on public bonds." Add in NBA, MLB, and NHL handouts and that figure soars even higher. Instead of adorning these new stadiums and arenas with corporate brands they should be called Taxpayer Stadium or Taxpayer Arena.

"The second Sports Tax comes in the form of a rigged tax code, which effectively compels honest taxpayers to bankroll professional teams," according to Sirota. He cites research that taxpayers subsidize at least $91 million worth of tax loopholes for pro sports leagues.

The third Sports Tax involves cable and satellite TV bills. Sirota refers to a *Los Angeles Times* story that says up to half of cable bill payments are for the sports services incorporated into most basic cable packages. Cable subscribers aren't allowed to opt out. As such, non–sports fans are forced to subsidize the sports fans who watch cable TV sports.

The fourth piece of this Sports Tax involves big-time college sports. We end up paying more taxes for higher education and higher tuition bills to help fund the athletic departments at major universities. These athletic departments have the advantage of operating under the nonprofit umbrella of their universities. Taxpayers are funding the incredible arms race we're experiencing in college sports—e.g., football coaches are now making $5 million-plus a year, and plush athletic dorms and workout facilities are popping up across our college campuses (see chapter 5, "College Sports: Where Do We Go from Here?).

Even the most ardent sports fans are beginning to agree that the Sports Tax has gotten out of hand, especially in this era of economic challenges and declining budgets for things like schools, police, and fire protection.

However, when it comes to pro sports, fans and taxpayers find themselves in an interesting predicament. Sports economist Andrew Zimbalist summarizes it this way:

"Demand for major league teams exceeds supply. Supply is restricted by a self-regulating monopoly. The inevitable result is that some worthy cities do not get teams and that the fortunate cities with teams are held hostage to threats of moving. This leads to the construction of new public stadiums filled with luxury boxes and elaborate electronic scoreboards, city guarantees on ticket sales, and heavily subsidized rent."

It's certainly not a new problem. This issue has been around for a long time. In his 1965 book, *The Hustler's Handbook*, Bill Veeck summarized the sad situation that was the Brooklyn Dodgers' move to Los Angeles in 1958:

> The Brooklyn Dodgers were a winning team and a profitable one. The Brooklyn fans supported the team when it was a loser, and they had supported it so well as a winner that over the previous decade the Dodgers had been second only to the Yankees in attendance and profitability.
>
> The Brooklyn fans had become the symbol of the baseball fanatic. They were recognized by ballplayers throughout the league as the most knowledgeable in the country. The Dodgers were a part of the [borough's] identification, a part of its pulse beat. The loyal rooters never doubted for a moment that

their beloved Bums were as much a part of their heritage as Prospect Park. They discovered they were wrong. The Dodgers were only a piece of merchandise that passed from hand to hand.

Until the 1960s, public works were often defined as bridges, roads, sewers, and so on: basic infrastructure that was used by all and was unlikely to be built by the private sector. The term "public works" didn't include massive stadiums and arenas for wealthy private owners of sports franchises. With few exceptions, for example, County Stadium in Milwaukee, teams constructed their own stadiums.

As pro sports expanded into cities from coast to coast (led by the Dodgers and Giants leaving New York for the gold that lured them to California), politicians and business leaders pushed for taxpayer-financed stadiums to attract teams. A couple of examples: New York built Shea Stadium for the expansion of the Mets, Atlanta put up Fulton County Stadium to attract the Braves from Milwaukee, and Oakland built a stadium to lure the Athletics from Kansas City. These were seen as the new "public works" projects.

Soon after, Philadelphia, Pittsburgh, and Cincinnati built stadiums for teams already based in those cities. In some cases, local political leaders justified the expense as a way to keep owners from moving their teams. At other times, politicians argued that the stadiums would generate enough revenue to cover the construction cost.

"Publicly funded sports stadiums are like crack cocaine to local politicians and business bigwigs," says Michael Lynch of *Reason* magazine. "These folks are just like addicts: They deceive everyone around them for the sake of a fix and rarely take no for an answer when voters decline to subsidize their schemes."

It's interesting to note that in a capitalist society in which team owners tout the free market whenever they can, it's a corporate welfare system—most notably taxpayer-financed sports stadiums and arenas—that is serving to help increase the wealth of pro sports owners in America.

"Ironically, it [taxpayer financing of sports venues] is a reverse type of socialism that redistributes wealth upward," says sports sociologist D. Stanley Eitzen. "Yet owners, civic boosters, editorial writers, and politicians who spend much of their time defending capitalism and the free market support it unabashedly and uncritically."

Sports economist Robert A. Baade calls it the Reverse Robin Hood Effect, "taking from the poor, the near poor, the working class, and the middle classes and giving to the rich."

Former president George W. Bush was a beneficiary of the Reverse Robin Hood Effect. In 1989 Bush invested $600,000 to become part owner of the American League's Texas Rangers. When the team was sold in 1998—four years after a new stadium was built for team owners by the city of Arlington, Bush earned a profit of at least $14.9 million from the deal according to CNN.

In 1993, while still playing in Municipal Stadium, the Cleveland Indians had a market value of $81 million. In 1994, when the new publicly subsidized Jacobs Field opened, the value of the team jumped to an estimated $100 million. By 1996 it was $125 million (a return of 54.3 percent for the Indians' owners in the three years following the opening of a new stadium built by taxpayers).

Today, due to pressures from opponents of taxpayer-financed stadiums, some new stadiums and arenas are financed in part by the franchise owners. However, these contributions are usually a fragment of the total costs for these sports palaces and are done mostly for public relations reasons and as a strategy for securing public dollars.

The public often pays 80 percent or more of the stadium/arena construction costs, along with other infrastructure costs around the stadium. In the vast majority of cases, the city, county, or stadium district owns the stadium/arena and leases it to the franchise owner for a very nominal fee. These sweetheart leases usually give owners various revenue streams, including parking and concessions revenue, stadium/arena naming-rights fees, and income from luxury suites, club seats, and personal seat licenses (PSLs).

Moreover, the revenue streams from the sweetheart leases offset any operations and maintenance costs the owners are responsible for, along with a big portion of any stadium/arena financing costs. So, even when the public is told franchise owners are paying for part of the cost of the new stadium, other revenue streams like naming rights significantly or completely offset those expenditures.

Of course, some communities are more blatant with their gifts, presenting a sparkling new sports stadium to the local pro sports franchise owner basically gratis. Consider Lucas Oil Stadium, home of the Indianapolis Colts. Costs for the new stadium exceeded original estimates, forcing the city to move more tax dollars toward the project. Moreover, the city even pays for operation and maintenance costs on the new stadium. So, for the privilege of having the Colts play ten games a year in their city, local taxpayers are stuck with a $700 million bill for the stadium and $20 million a year for operations and maintenance. That's a lot of green for the wealthy owners of a team that thousands of local taxpayers couldn't care less about.

In effect taxpayers in these publicly financed stadium deals take on virtually all the risk (including the responsibility for cost overruns) without any financial upside.

"The public, which invested most of the money for construction and maintenance of the facility, receives none of the proceeds," says Eitzen.

On rare occasions, when opposition efforts are strong enough and unified, these taxpayer-financed stadium schemes can be successfully fought. In the late 1990s Robert Kraft, owner of the New England Patriots, was close to getting approximately $500 million from Connecticut taxpayers for a new stadium in downtown Hartford. Opposition groups, led by Ralph Nader and the Connecticut Green Party, filed a lawsuit against the proposed stadium and rallied opposition. Ultimately, Kraft backed out of the Hartford deal, seeing the tough road ahead due to opposition efforts.

In most cases, however, stadium proponents, often led by a community's most influential politicians, muffle opposition efforts by touting the community benefits of a new stadium or arena.

What exactly does the community get for its multimillion dollar investment? The franchise owners, along with the local politicians that pull the strings for the public financing of new stadiums and arenas, claim that new stadiums and arenas create jobs in the local community.

However, there are very few new jobs created beyond a minimal number of low-paying part-time jobs. The number of full-time equivalent (FTE) jobs is very small. The gross and net job gains are pathetically small, especially given the level of public investment and the few games played over the course of a year. In fact economist Roger Noll believes the estimated jobs effect of a subsidized sports facility is actually negative because spending at the stadium substitutes for spending elsewhere for which a greater number of people are employed per dollar spent.

What else does the community get for its huge investment? A chance to keep the team in town for another ten to fifteen years, at which point the pro sports owner will likely demand a refurbished, or new, stadium and threaten to leave town if the demand isn't met.

As Neil deMause, author of *Field of Schemes*, says, "The only thing limiting how soon owners will ask for a new stadium is chutzpah."

The NFL's Atlanta Falcons pressured city political leaders to consent to tearing down the Georgia Dome, a twenty-year-old stadium, for a new $1 billion-plus retractable roof stadium with greater revenue streams.

The thirty-year-old Metrodome, home of the NFL's Minnesota Vikings, was torn down in February 2014 to make way for a new stadium, which is projected to open in 2016. Minnesota taxpayers will be stuck with more than 50 percent of the construction costs. Moreover, stadium naming rights were given to the team and PSLs will be used to get fans to pay part of the Vikings' share of construction costs.

An underreported fact is that taxpayers also get stuck paying for stadiums and arenas long after the local pro sports team has finished playing in them.

In 2010 New Jersey taxpayers still owed $110 million in debt on bonds for the old Giants stadium. The old Giants stadium was demolished and turned into a parking lot for the Giants' new facility, MetLife Stadium. New Jersey taxpayers are joined by taxpayers in Seattle, Indianapolis, Houston, Kansas City, Memphis, and Pittsburgh, all cities still paying for stadiums or arenas that no longer host a pro sports franchise.

Being a pro sports owner is one of the sweetest of all investments—at least in the NFL, MLB, and NBA. Several years back, former New York Yankee, author, and sports activist Jim Bouton described just how sweet a deal it is when talking about MLB owners:

> Who's got a better deal than baseball owners? You have no factories, no raw materials, no inventory and no technological obsolescence in a monopoly business that binds your employees to you for the first six years after they're hired. The media give you free publicity, the taxpayers build the stadiums and the players provide the labor.

THE MIAMI MARLINS: A PARTICULARLY UGLY CASE STUDY

Jeffrey Loria, owner of Major League Baseball's (MLB) Miami Marlins, continues to use and abuse city and county taxpayers. First, while fielding lousy teams for years with one of the lowest payrolls in baseball, he threatened to move the Marlins if his demands for a sweetheart stadium deal weren't met. Second, just one year after local politicians gave him his new stadium in 2012, he dumped all the expensive big-name players on his team, several of them on the roster for only one year, reducing his payroll costs significantly.

By 2013 Marlins fans once again had one of the worst teams in the big leagues. They also have a stadium to pay off, one that will cost them approximately $2.4 billion over forty years. Loria gets basically every revenue stream from the new ballpark, including naming rights, concessions, and ticket sales (even ticket sales from non-baseball events like soccer games and concerts). For this, Loria only had to spend $120 million for construction costs and $2 million in annual loan repayments. That's pure thievery.

The ballpark financing scheme, between Loria, other Marlins executives, and local politicians, was so shady that it resulted in an SEC investigation.

"I think it's a fair deal for the community and a fair deal for the Marlins," said MLB president and COO Bob DuPuy.

Now that's a strange sense of fairness. Local taxpayers didn't agree with DuPuy's assessment. Miami–Dade County voters pushed out Mayor Carlos Alvarez in a recall election on March 15, 2011. Alvarez was a vocal proponent of the new ballpark and pushed for a higher property-tax rate. Alvarez's manager, George Burgess, who helped engineer the deal, and county commissioner Natacha Seijas were also recalled, for similar reasons. Former commissioner Carlos Giminez, a critic of the new stadium scheme, won election as county mayor after a special election on June 28, 2011.

"Miami has a history of bad deals, but I would rank this Number 1," according to current city of Miami mayor Tomas Regalado. "The residents of Miami were raped. Completely."

Regalado was also a vocal critic of the stadium deal and observers believe his stadium opposition was a big factor in his being elected mayor. "This is the most despised ownership I've ever seen in this town," says Giminez. "They took the county for a ride to get a stadium. They've taken the people for a ride with the product they've put out."

Loria cried poor when lobbying for the new stadium, even though a *Forbes* report said the Marlins turned a $43.7 million profit in 2008. Meanwhile, the franchise refused to open its books to city officials—and local politicians in bed with Loria refused to demand it.

"In Major League Baseball history, books are just kept private," said David Samson, president of the Marlins and former stepson of Loria's. "That's just how it is."

Those same politicians who never asked to see the Marlins' books also never put the new stadium to a referendum so taxpayers could vote on it. "You are talking about an ownership group that lied to the public and came away with hundreds of millions of dollars on the basis of those lies," says activist sports journalist Dave Zirin. "And instead of paying a penalty, they've been rewarded. It's all from the public till."

While taxpayers in Florida are on the hook for $2.4 billion for Loria's play palace, Loria is doing just fine, thank you. His initial $15 million MLB investment in 1999 has turned into a Marlins franchise worth $450 million, according to *Forbes*.

"The brazen looting of the public treasury, of funds that otherwise could pay for schools, roads and cops and hospitals, by selfish, toy-owning millionaires who don't even need the money—isn't simply Florida's problem," says sports culture writer Patrick Hruby. "It's America's problem, too."

PRO SPORTS LEAGUES: GOVERNMENT-SANCTIONED SPORTS CARTELS

Publicly financed stadiums and arenas are an issue because of the ill-conceived public policy at their foundation.

In his book *Playing Hardball: The High Stakes Battle for Baseball's New Franchises*, David Whitford talks about the ramifications of a sports policy that allows for a government-sanctioned, unregulated sports cartel. His comments were in regard to MLB but could just as easily apply to the other major professional sports leagues in the United States.

"For as long as baseball is free to operate as an unregulated cartel, as long as it can sustain a high level of unsatisfied demand for its product, as long as cities have no choice but to compete suicidally with one another to try and attract and later hold onto franchises, then baseball wins and everybody else loses, in a hundred different ways: stadiums are built with tax dollars, roads and other components of the infrastructure are improved for private gain at community expense, and revenue streams are diverted from the public purse into owners' pockets," wrote Whitford.

Highly respected sports economist Roger Noll blames this situation on the various antitrust protections that pro sports leagues enjoy.

"We are just pointing out two important facts," says Noll. "Stadiums are not a net local economic benefit, and the reasons cities are paying for them is because the (federal) government made the professional leagues monopolies exempt from anti-trust laws that apply to most other industries."

Consumer advocate Gene Kimmelman discussed some of the ethical problems the current system breeds when addressing MLB's antitrust exemption:

> Hidden behind our national pastime's positive cultural image is a pattern of questionable business practices, peculiar (and possibly extortionist) expansion and franchise transfer decisions, volatile labor relations and anti-consumer television contracts that are shielded from antitrust scrutiny.

Zimbalist, in testimony before the Senate Subcommittee on Antitrust, Monopolies and Business Rights, said the lack of checks and balances in professional sports is the big problem.

"In other cases where the government has deemed it desirable to sanction a monopoly, such as with public utilities, the government has also sought to assure through regulatory controls that the monopoly did not abuse its privileges," says Zimbalist.

Not so with our pro sports leagues. They continue to operate as self-governing, unregulated monopolies. There is no minister of sports, sports regulatory agency, or sports policy commission in the United States.

The majority of American businesses, which face the limitations of either legitimate competition or regulation, need to be responsive to several stakeholder groups in order to simply survive as business entities. However, American public policy concerning pro sports is heavily weighted in favor of only one stakeholder group, the owners of the franchises, who have been blessed with numerous political and economic advantages.

Sports policy expert Evan Weiner outlines some of the political advantages bestowed by government and enjoyed by NFL owners:

> The NFL clearly has been built by Congress: the Sports Broadcasting Act of 1961, the 1966 AFL-NFL merger, the 1984 cable TV bill that allowed cable operators to bundle channels on a basic tier and forced subscribers to pay for all channels on a basic tier—the tier that became the home to sports—whether the subscribers watch sports programming or not, and the 1986 tax code revision which changed the way municipally-funded stadiums and arenas were financed and placed the burden of paying off the debt on taxpayers and helped along by local elected officials.

While testifying before Congress during an antitrust hearing in 1993, former MLB commissioner Fay Vincent addressed the fact that baseball is a sociocultural institution, not just a business, and therefore needs to be treated differently: "Ownership of a baseball team is more than ownership of an ordinary business. Owners have a duty to take into consideration that they own a part of America's national pastime in trust. This trust sometimes requires putting self-interest second. . . . Only a strong commissioner acting in the interests of baseball, and therefore, the public, can protect the institution from the selfish and myopic attitudes of owners."

Wow. Vincent nailed it. However, in 1992, MLB owners decided that having a commissioner operate in the "best interests of the game" wasn't in *their* best interests. As such, they forced Vincent out and put a fellow owner, Bud Selig, in the commissioner's chair to protect their PAAC interests.

After all, a cartel's basic purpose is maximizing profits for the members of its protected venture. And from the owners' perspective, they sure didn't want a commissioner who was concerned about protecting the best interests of the game or looking out for the fans at the expense of maximizing profits.

Political science professor Charles Euchner sums up the primary issue with pro sports this way: "At no time in modern debates over the development of sports policy has the fundamental character of the industry been questioned."

It's time to begin some serious questioning. We need a better system. The current foundational structure of pro sports in this country is deeply flawed.

THERE IS A BETTER WAY: COMMUNITY OWNERSHIP

The best town in pro sports is also the smallest: Green Bay, Wisconsin, home of the Packers. The Dallas Cowboys aren't America's team, the Green Bay Packers are.

The Packers are owned by the fans, not a wealthy owner/corporation operating with a PAAC philosophy. The Green Bay Packers are a publicly owned nonprofit with a unique stock ownership structure.

The Packers issued stock to the public in 1923 in order to stay afloat as a franchise. Ownership pays no dividends and doesn't provide any other perks. (Most notably, there aren't any game-ticket privileges!) The Packers have conducted a few additional rounds of stock sales since 1923. Today, the franchise has 112,158 shareholders who own 4.7 million shares. Most shareholders live in the Green Bay area, or at least in the state of Wisconsin, although there are no residency requirements. Nevertheless, all profits are invested back into the team.

Green Bay's bylaws state that the Packers are "a community project, intended to promote community welfare." What a refreshing concept.

"It makes them an example," according to sports and culture writer Patrick Hruby. "A case study. A working model for a better way to organize and administer pro sports."

What would the NFL have looked like if every franchise had been owned through a Packers-like model since 1960?

"The upshot?" asks Hruby. "Had the Baltimore Colts' ownership structure been similar to Green Bay's, they never would have left in overnight trucks for Indianapolis. The Cleveland Browns never would have left for Baltimore. The Seattle Sonics never would have jetted to Oklahoma City. Los Angeles might still have an NFL team. Or two."

The Green Bay model works.

"Green Bay is a dangerous example for [sports] owners," contends Dave Zirin, a leading sports journalist/activist. "Because the franchise proves the argument for public ownership in practice."

Michael N. Danielson, in his book *Home Team: Professional Sports and the American Metropolis*, writes, "Professional team sports in the United States and Canada have always been rooted in places. Major league teams have fostered close identification with the urban areas where they played, and sports fans are primarily interested in the fortunes of their home team."

Due to the close identification a city's fans have with their local teams and the prestige and civic self-esteem that pro sports franchises can some-times bring a community, the stakes are high for cities when they play the "pro sports game." Cities compete for the limited number of pro sports teams available. They fight to acquire sports franchises and make a con-certed effort to protect the ones they currently have.

"Threats to relocate arouse public concern largely because of the emo-tional and symbolic connections between teams, places and people," ac-cording to Danielson.

As a result, for the last half century, pro sports' wealthy owners have taken advantage of the economic and political advantages we've given them as a society, along with the loyalty and close identification fans have with pro sports franchises, to secure new sports palaces with little out-of-pocket expense on their part.

The clear answer to this situation is community ownership. However, pro sports owners recognized the threat that community ownership repre-sented to their golden goose decades ago and formally and informally took steps against community ownership. In fact, Pete Rozelle changed the NFL constitution in 1960 to try to prevent another Green Bay Packers owner-ship situation. Article V, Section 4 of the NFL constitution, the "Green Bay Rule," says that "charitable organizations and/or corporations not organized for profit and not now a member of the league may not hold membership in the National Football League."

The NFL owners said no to community ownership because they can. They're free to establish any policies they'd like. They're a *self-regulated* monopoly, blessed by our government with great profits, while taking al-most zero risk.

"Why should the great unwashed enjoy any of the money-printing, antitrust-exempted fun?" asks Hruby.

MLB owners have also shot down community ownership. In the 1980s Joan Kroc offered to donate the San Diego Padres to San Diego, plus $100 million for operating expenses. The owners killed the idea even though a transfer of ownership like that is not specifically banned in MLB's bylaws. MLB also prevented the cities of Montreal and Quebec from buying the Expos. Their rationale? MLB has said that such arrangements would be "awkward."

"Awkward" for MLB owners means they don't want financial information to become public, as would be the case under a community ownership model, because that would hurt their position in negotiating collective bargaining agreements and new stadium deals. Of course, that would be to the benefit of fans and taxpayers, who suffer from the greed and PAAC policies and decisions inherent in the current self-regulated monopoly system.

Ewing Kauffman and the Kansas City Royals came up with an alternative way to tie a franchise to a particular city. Kauffman donated the team to charity in 1995 with two conditions: (1) the charitable foundation had to sell it to someone who would commit to keeping the team in Kansas City; and (2) the proceeds from the sale had to go to local Kansas City charities. The IRS (and, somewhat surprisingly, MLB) approved this ownership transfer. This arrangement doesn't call for pure community ownership. However, it does seemingly tie the team permanently to Kansas City, although the model hasn't been legally challenged.

While the Green Bay Packers remain the only *major* professional sports team with a community ownership structure, there are plenty of minor league examples in professional sports:

- The Wisconsin Timber Rattlers are a Class A baseball team. They are structured as a nonprofit in a similar fashion to the Green Bay Packers. They pump all proceeds back into the team and stadium.
- The Harrisburg Senators AA baseball team is owned by Harrisburg, Pennsylvania. The city paid $6.5 million in 1995 to save the team for the local community. The previous owners were planning to move the team to Massachusetts.
- The Memphis Redbirds, a AAA baseball franchise, are structured as a nonprofit charitable organization. Owner Dean Jernigan spent $8 million in 1997 to bring the team to town and then turned it over to a foundation. "If the main identity of a city is tied to a sports team, who are we going to entrust this to?" asks Jernigan. "Who can be responsible? It's not an individual I can assure you."
- The Rochester Red Wings and Syracuse SkyChiefs are AAA teams in New York state. They became fan-owned teams via stock offerings in the 1950s, when their major league affiliates cut financial support to the teams.

- The Toledo Mud Hens, made famous by Corporal Klinger in the television show *M*A*S*H*, have been part of Toledo's heritage since 1883. However, in 1952 an outside investor bought the team and moved the franchise to Charleston, West Virginia. Another team moved to Toledo for three years before moving to Wichita, Kansas. In 1965 frustrated civic leaders created the Toledo Mud Hens Baseball Club, a nonprofit corporation, and with financial backing from Lucas County, acquired the Richmond, Virginia, franchise. The team has a permanent home now in Toledo, Ohio.

RECOMMENDATIONS

The first three recommendations are proposed for the current situation: privately owned professional sports franchises. The fourth recommendation proposes an overhaul of the current system and a transition to a community-based ownership structure.

The first three recommendations allow fans to claim their rightful partnership with owners and force the owners to be accountable to the fans. The partnership claim is based on the fact that in the vast majority of cases, fans, as taxpayers, are responsible for the stadiums and arenas the owners use to make money. Taxpayers are also responsible for the numerous infrastructural amenities and improvements around the stadiums and arenas that owners leverage. Moreover, the fan/ownership partnership claim is also based on the sweetheart leases that cities, counties, and stadium districts provide owners, resulting in a variety of lucrative revenue streams for team owners.

"In any tax-supported sports facility, the fans should become shareholders because they're taxpayers," says League of Fans' Ralph Nader. "There should be organized fans' groups that can sit at the table. Anything that intersects public policy with the sports teams, the fans have got to have representatives at the table."

I. No TV Blackouts on Games Broadcast from Publicly Financed Sports Venues

Fans in cities with professional sports franchises should be entitled to television access to all home games if the stadium has been built with public funds. Therefore, legislation needs to be enacted that disallows any blackouts of sporting events from stadiums and arenas built with local taxpayer dollars. This includes stadiums and arenas that are both fully funded and partially funded with taxpayer financing.

2. Profit Sharing for Cities That Have Publicly Financed Sports Venues

Cities that have subsidized pro sports franchises with publicly financed stadiums/arenas and other forms of corporate sports welfare should receive a percentage of profits resulting from a sale of the local professional sports franchise. This arrangement should be made a condition of owners accepting public funding for stadium/arena construction. Since owners benefit from the appreciation in the club's value over time, while the publicly financed stadium simultaneously depreciates in value, taxpayers should be allowed to share in the appreciation of the franchise, if and when it's sold—even if it's sold to a local private buyer who contractually agrees to keep the team in town.

3. Establish Fan/Taxpayer Councils

For franchises utilizing taxpayer-financed stadiums and arenas, fan/taxpayer rights are naturally established. As such, fans and taxpayers should be represented, in the form of fan/taxpayer councils, during franchise policy-making deliberations.

A New Model

4. Community Ownership: A Three-Step Plan for Tying Professional Sports Franchises to Communities through a Community Ownership Structure

Pro sports franchises are important to communities financially, socially, culturally, and emotionally. As previously discussed, followers of sports franchises identify with "their teams" in ways they don't with any other business in their communities. Pro sports teams provide a common link for members of a community, regardless of race, income, or what part of town one lives in. As such, it's important that we, as a society, find a way to prevent franchise owners from playing "franchise free agency" and re-locating—or threatening to relocate—around the country in quest of the next sweetheart stadium or arena deal.

To that end, the New Rules Project of the Institute for Local Self-Reliance offers a compelling three-part remedy to the current self-regulated monopoly structure in professional sports:

Step One is to overturn professional sports leagues' ban on community/fan ownership. This will most likely require congressional action. Representative Earl Blumenauer's (D-Oregon) "Give Fans a Chance Act," introduced in the 107th Congress, provides a solid model. (The bill, H.R. 3257, was introduced in the House of Representatives on November 8, 2001. It died before becoming law.).

According to David Morris of the New Rules Project, something like the "Give Fans a Chance Act" is a good starting point:

> The bill would forbid any of the professional leagues from prohibiting community ownership, and would withdraw the leagues' antitrust privileges if they did so. It also requires teams to give their communities 180 days notice of proposed relocation, during which time the community can put together an offer to retain the franchise. Lastly, it requires that leagues consider factors such as fan loyalty and whether the community is opposed to the move before approving relocation.

This type of legislation would open the door to community ownership at the big-league level. The community ownership model of the Green Bay Packers works. It needs to become an option for communities.

"The nonprofit team (Green Bay Packers) is financially solvent, competitive, and deeply connected to the community," writes Dave Zirin in *Bad Sports: How Owners Are Ruining the Games We Love*. "It has created something beautiful: a throwback that is also forward-looking. It deserves to be replicated."

Legislation like the "Give Fans a Chance Act" would be a significant step forward for fans across America because community/fan ownership permanently roots teams in their communities and strengthens the bond between a team and its fans.

Zimbalist supports an ownership right-of-first-refusal policy that could result in more Green Bay Packer-like ownership structures. "Before an owner was allowed to move a team or to sell it to owners in another city, the team should be offered for sale to its host city," argues Zimbalist.

The ownership right-of-first-refusal policy would protect fans in a couple of ways. If the current owner wanted to sell or move the franchise, the local community could step in and buy the franchise at a fair appraised value and either run the franchise, find a local buyer who would agree to keep the franchise in the city, create a foundation to operate the team, or sell it to fans via a stock offering.

The "community/fan ownership" concept would be similar to "plant-closing legislation" passed in 1988. This legislation was designed to give workers of failing companies a "window of opportunity" to take over the failed company before it folded or moved. As part of a right-of-first-refusal policy in pro sports, a plant-closing legislation type of clause could be applicable for fans in cases where their city's pro sports franchise is failing and/or threatening to move. Under a proposal of this nature, a city and/or its fans would have a reasonable, specified period to purchase a franchise whose intent is to leave for another locale.

Policies like those discussed here would prevent the sudden departure of franchises from cities with a long history of franchise support (e.g., Oakland Raiders to Los Angeles; Baltimore Colts to Indianapolis; Cleveland Browns to Baltimore; Brooklyn Dodgers to Los Angeles).

Step Two requires Congress to extend the NFL's revenue-sharing program to MLB, the NBA, and the NHL. Community-based ownership isn't sufficient without NFL-like revenue sharing.

"Despite their storied fan support, the Green Bay Packers would have folded or moved long ago if not for the revenue-sharing agreement of the NFL, which distributes revenues from merchandise sales, broadcasting and a portion of gate receipts evenly among all teams," according to David Morris, cofounder of the Institute for Local Self-Reliance. "Without such sharing, small-town teams could not survive. The NFL rightly understood that the media revenue comes in large part because of the parity the league has achieved since revenue sharing. Such parity has not occurred in the other sports leagues where the team with the biggest payroll usually wins."

Michael N. Danielson, author of *Home Team*, concurs with this approach: "Places would benefit if professional sports leagues shared all revenues; and Congress should require that leagues share revenues."

Step Three would require "mandated expansion" for cities that lose a well-supported, publicly subsidized franchise due to the whims of an owner who decides to move the franchise to another city.

In short, if a franchise owner wants to sell or relocate, and the local community/fan base isn't interested in purchasing the franchise at market value—or isn't currently prepared to—and a local buyer can't be found, the franchise would be allowed to move. However, if the local community had been supportive of the franchise based on a set of established criteria, e.g., strong attendance (as was the case with the Cleveland Browns), the league would be required to expand back into that community within a short time frame if the community comes up with a viable community ownership plan or a local private owner is found.

The Browns were yanked from Cleveland and moved to Baltimore by owner Art Modell despite years of outstanding attendance and other community support for the franchise. The team was making a handsome profit in Cleveland. Modell was enticed to move by the huge public subsidies being offered by Baltimore, which had lost its team, the Colts, to Indianapolis less than twenty years before. Cleveland would definitely have qualified for mandated expansion under this proposal.

If this "mandated expansion" step was implemented, leagues and franchise owners would have to consider the trade-off between increasing a particular franchise's value in the short term (via franchise relocation) versus the long-term consequence of average team values dropping across the league due to expanding the number of teams in the league because of the mandated expansion clause. Due to a mandated expansion clause, league owners would have to share television revenue with a lot more teams (mandated expansion franchises) if they allowed league franchises to relocate around the country.

This three-step plan would go a long way toward keeping franchises from relocating for quick profit gains derived from moving to publicly subsidized stadiums/arenas in other cities. It would also eliminate the leverage franchise owners have to extract for new stadiums/arenas and improvements from their current community's taxpayers.

As Morris says, this strategy would ensure that our children, grandchildren, and beyond would "have the opportunity to root, root, root for a team that is truly rooted" in its community.

Just like the Green Bay Packers.

CONCUSSION RESEARCH DEMANDS NEW POLICIES

Too many sports organizations, from the little leagues to the professional level, continue to have their heads in the sand when it comes to concussion safety and prevention measures. The growing mound of research showing the often devastating long-term effects of sports-related brain trauma demands that we take vigorous measures to protect our young athletes' brains.

Ralph Nader, founder, League of Fans

Ann McKee is a neuropathologist and a leading brain concussion researcher. When asked how she'd advise her nineteen-year-old son if he was offered a chance to play in the NFL, she said, "I'd say, 'Don't. Not if you want to have a life after football.'"

And that's coming from a longtime, die-hard Green Bay Packers fan.

Being a sports fan is all about emotion and passion. Enjoying playing or watching football is one thing. Objectively, looking at all the research on football-induced brain trauma is a completely different thing.

One of the unfortunate outcomes of win-at-all-costs (WAAC) and profit-at-all-costs (PAAC) policies and decisions in SportsWorld is that safety concerns too often take a backseat to winning and making money.

One of the most glaring examples of this is with concussions and brain trauma issues. Historically, NFL, college, and high school players have been encouraged to shake off concussions and get back on the field. Coaches and trainers have historically told players that they've simply had their "bell rung," and that apart from a few cobwebs, everything is fine. Pass the smelling salts.

Part of the NFL culture—and to a lesser degree SportsWorld in general—is the pressure to "play hurt." As a result, most former NFL players have chronic debilitating conditions of one degree or another, most of which can be traced to a football injury.

Unfortunately, the suck-it-up, "just play through it" approach to injuries in sports has seeped down to the youth sports level where overuse injuries for boys and girls are nearing epidemic proportions. The "Be tough!" mentality rules the day. The problem is "Be tough!" doesn't work with brain injuries.

What we've learned about brain injuries demands that we take the subject of safety in sports to an entirely different level. If the injury is a sprained ankle or tendonitis, that's one thing; it's another thing if it's a brain concussion. What makes the diagnosis and treatment of concussions especially tough is that people can't see brain injuries with the naked eye like they can a sprained ankle.

"Everyone says, 'You look fine, why can't you play?' You're dealing with a macho, heavy-testosterone sport," says pro football agent Peter Schaffer.

"When I first started investigating concussions, I found that everything we were doing in sports was wrong when it came to the brain," says Chris Nowinski, codirector of the Center for the Study of Traumatic Encephalopathy at Boston University School of Medicine. "I discovered we weren't diagnosing concussions properly; athletes weren't resting long enough after concussions; we were allowing too much brain trauma that could have been avoided; and there weren't any return-to-play guidelines in place, to name a few things."

Undoubtedly, the most important safety and injury prevention issue in sports today is concussions and repetitive head trauma. Arguably, it's the most important contemporary sports issue overall. Getting your "bell rung" is nothing to be taken lightly; it is serious stuff—especially at the high school and youth levels where developing brains are more vulnerable.

"I believe the most important issue by far is brain trauma, especially when you consider the huge number of children participating in sports," says sports journalist Patrick Hruby. "Children's brains are still developing. Brain trauma at young ages can have lasting negative effects.

"Brain trauma in youth sports, especially football, is both a scientific and moral issue. A recent study showed that the impact of hits in youth football have the same impact as hits in college football."

At the end of 2010, NFL commissioner Roger Goodell, along with a mix of NFL executives, doctors, players, and members of Congress, took part in a House Judiciary Committee hearing on football-induced brain concussions.

You may or may not think Congress is overstepping its bounds by inquiring into the NFL's policies on concussions, but one thing is certain: How the NFL deals with concussions has a big impact on how college, high school, and youth football organizations deal with head injuries.

As such, the congressional hearings on concussions brought needed attention to an issue impacting the safety of our young athletes. (It's not just a football issue; girls' soccer is second to football in number of concussions, and many other sports have a significant amount of concussions as well. However, football represents the most serious problem, not just because of the number of reported concussions, but also because of the suspected number of concussions that don't get reported and because of the repetitive subconcussive blows to the head inherent in the sport. Moreover, football is the lone high school sport in which inflicting physical punishment on one's opponent is a primary objective.)

Julian Bailes, a prominent neurosurgeon, is extremely upset with the NFL on the issue of brain trauma, not just because of what it means to its own employees but what it means for football players at the college, high school, and youth levels. "Here we have a multibillion-dollar industry," says Bailes. "Where does their responsibility begin? Say you're a kid and you sign up to play football. You realize you can blow out your knee, you can even break your neck and become paralyzed. Those are all known risks. But you don't sign up to become a brain-damaged young adult. The NFL should be leading the world in figuring this out, acknowledging the risk. They should be thanking us for bringing them this research."

THE CONCUSSION SITUATION AT THE COLLEGE LEVEL IS WORSE THAN AT THE PRO LEVEL

The different ways in which a commercial sports league addresses serious head injuries can vary between corporate responsibility and callous barbarism.

The NFL has received a lot of heat recently for how it has handled concussions—most of it well deserved—but the NFL's current policy is much better than the laissez-faire approach of the National Collegiate Athletic Association (NCAA). Despite all the research in recent years on brain damage from concussions in sports—particularly in football—the NCAA does not yet have a comprehensive policy on the subject for its member schools, only "general guidelines," which were issued well after the serious long-term effects of concussions were known.

"The NCAA, for years, turned a blind eye to the concussion problem and never addressed the issue," says Joseph Siprut, an attorney who filed a class action lawsuit against the NCAA in September 2011.

Siprut says his lawsuit is focusing on the NCAA because its officials knew as early as 2003 that multiple concussions could lead to health problems, yet did not ask colleges to have concussion policies until 2010. In the suit, he claims the NCAA isn't adequately protecting football players and other student-athletes from brain trauma, including concussions. According to Siprut, the NCAA's concussion policy only really says that every member school has to have their own concussion management plan.

"In practice, that's led to complete disaster," says Siprut. "The problem is that left to their own devices, the schools aren't really addressing the issue consistently and effectively. There's no consistency. As a result, these brain trauma issues have been exacerbated and increased in number far beyond the point that they should have."

The NCAA Compliance Manual states that member schools should (a) inform athletes about the signs and symptoms of concussions; (b) remove athletes who show signs of a concussion from play; and (c) prohibit students from returning to play the same day they were initially injured.

That's it. The manual doesn't mention limits on contact in practice. No guidelines on detecting and screening brain injuries. No comprehensive return-to-play policy for athletes suffering from brain trauma. And, most importantly, there are no consequences if a member school fails to come up with a plan and enforce it. It amounts to just partial exhortations.

"A lot of schools simply don't do a good job of addressing the issue," says Siprut. "There's no consistency. If there were more effective measures in place, it would certainly help student-athletes. Failure to do so is negligence."

It seems clear the NCAA has delegated the concussion issue to schools as a strategy to avoid any legal liability and potential financial losses. All at the expense of their student-athletes' health and safety. Meanwhile, the NCAA rakes in billions of dollars from television and other sources.

The NCAA's lack of leadership in this area is especially troubling because college athletes lack meaningful representation. They don't have a union to fight for their best interests. Their health and safety is at the mercy of the NCAA and the big-time business interests of college sports.

"What strikes me about the two different situations is that at the NFL level the players at least have some kind of representation," says Siprut.

"They've got agents, they've got full lobbying for their interests through the union, and in many cases they're making millions of dollars a year.

"At the NCAA level, they're just kids, they're just playing the sport for fun; some are on scholarship and some aren't. And there's really no one looking out for their interests and no one representing them. The NCAA, which is supposed to be representing them, uses them up and spits them out."

In short, the NCAA has failed to adequately educate and protect college athletes on this issue. This avoidance behavior is especially troublesome given the fact that athlete safety was the primary reason the organization was formed. In the early 1900s, Theodore Roosevelt convened two conferences at the White House with college presidents to discuss the growing number of gruesome injuries and deaths occurring in college football. Those conferences resulted in the formation of the Intercollegiate Athletic Association of the United States (IAAUS) in 1906, which led to several safety-related policies and rules. (The IAAUS would become the NCAA in 1910.)

Now, over a century later, it appears we might once again need a presidential or congressional intervention to ensure the safety and health of unprotected college football players.

To avoid an unnecessary political intervention, the NCAA *must* do what it was formed to do: protect college athletes. It should implement *and* enforce strict return-to-play standards for players suspected of having concussions or brain trauma of any kind. It should also limit contact during practices, require independent concussion specialists to be present during games, and educate student-athletes in all contact sports about the potential degenerative brain conditions associated with those sports.

It's time for the NCAA to step up and take a serious approach to concussions and begin to accept its responsibility in the area of player safety.

"A uniform and consistent policy on the concussion issue is way overdue," says Siprut. "The concussion issue is the number one issue in sports, certainly in football. There's really no excuse to be moving this slow on it."

THE "LITTLE" HITS TO THE HEAD ADD UP TOO

It's not just full-blown concussions that are a cause for concern. Perhaps the most important recent finding in the area of concussion research is that repetitive small hits to the head can cause as much damage as big blows.

The University of North Carolina tracks the numbers of hits to the head the players in their football program take during a season, including games and practices. The average is 950 blows to the head each season. That's an important number because researchers are discovering that it's not just the major blows to the head that are dangerous. They all count.

Neuroscientist Kevin Guskiewicz believes that repetitive low-impact hits are enough to cause cumulative damage to young brain tissue but not enough to cause immediate symptoms.

"There's what we call a dose response," Guskiewicz says. "After a certain number of hits, the damage starts to show."

Dr. Robert Cantu, a leading expert on concussions and their long-term effects, concurs, saying "repetitive subconcussive trauma" adds up to long-term problems. This could apply to the constant head-banging that takes place between offensive and defensive linemen in football, as well as years and years of headers in soccer, regular head blows received in boxing and hockey, or any other sports situation in which there's repetitive subconcussive trauma.

Purdue researchers recently compared changes in the brains of high school football players who had suffered concussions with the brains of players who were concussion free and found brain tissue damage in both. That's scary stuff. That means brain injuries are occurring without concussions and without players, coaches, or parents being aware of it.

CTE: THE LONG-TERM IMPACT OF BRAIN TRAUMA

A growing concern in the brain trauma field is chronic traumatic encephalopathy (CTE), a degenerative brain disease. CTE, which is basically the same as "punch-drunk syndrome," has been an affliction tied to boxers since the 1920s.

For decades, boxing officials, fans, and reporters have too often ignored the impact of "knockouts" on boxers' health. Boxing, of course, is the ultimate sport for concussions. The goal is to knock out your opponent, in effect, to give the other person a serious concussion. Boxers are repeatedly sent back into action after being staggered with blows to the head.

Today, boxing is a niche sport in this country, with sagging popularity. As such, football and hockey have moved to the forefront when the subject of concussions in sports is brought up. Hockey superstars Eric Lindros and Sidney Crosby have suffered multiple concussions and have struggled, battling postconcussion syndrome. Their high-profile cases have softened attitudes toward head injuries in the macho culture of hockey.

However, football, due to its mass popularity, combined with recent publicity on concussions and their long-term impact on former NFL players, has become the primary focus of discussions regarding sports-related concussions.

"Football is the current poster child for [CTE]," according to H. Hunt Batjer, a Northwestern University neurosurgeon who cochairs the National Football League's Head, Neck, and Spine Committee.

In an October 2009 *New Yorker* article on brain injuries in football, author Malcolm Gladwell pointed out that CTE usually appears later in life because it takes a long time for the initial trauma to give rise to nerve-cell breakdown and death. CTE has many symptoms similar to Alzheimer's disease, however, it isn't the result of some endogenous disease but due to brain injury—being hit too many times in the head.

So, football players who retire from their sport believing that all their faculties are in order and that they've avoided long-term brain problems aren't necessarily out of the woods yet.

A neuropathologist named Bennet Omalu has only once failed to find CTE in the autopsies of more than twenty professional football players. Due to CTE brain disease, various cognitive and psychological problems among former pro football players may be more prevalent than neuroscientists currently believe.

Consider that the number of former NFL players between the ages thirty and forty-nine—*thirty and forty-nine!*—who have received diagnoses of "dementia, Alzheimer's disease, or other memory-related disease" is nineteen times the national average for that age group. Moreover, Guskiewicz found that players who had suffered multiple concussions were three times more likely to suffer depression.

"Brain trauma not only destroys the lives of some players, it destroys the lives of the people around them," says Hruby.

Ted Johnson played a decade for the New England Patriots as a hard-hitting linebacker. He was a Super Bowl hero who took thousands of hits to his brain. He retired due to a variety of effects from multiple concussions and repetitive subconcussive trauma. He became depressed. He was a drug addict. He seldom left his room. He was diagnosed with postconcussion syndrome by Dr. Cantu and told that by his fifties he could have severe Alzheimer's.

"Sometimes I wish Junior would have just blown his knees out and couldn't walk," says his father, Ted Johnson Sr. "But his brain? Oh, boy."

Football's challenge in making the sport safe for brains is ultimately greater than hockey's, or any other sport.

"I think we need to get rid of fighting in hockey," says Hruby. "That said, I do see more hope for hockey long-term than football. We can get rid of checking or at least make it a lot less physical, for example. Hockey doesn't have to involve massive amounts of physical contact to remain essentially the same game.

"On the other hand, you can't get rid of the physical aspects of football and have it remain essentially the same thing. If you try, it becomes flag football."

A study published in the scientific journal *Brain* at the end of 2012 strengthened the case that repetitive head trauma can lead to "long-term, degenerative brain disease."

The study took brain samples posthumously from eighty-five people who had histories of repeated mild traumatic brain injury. The results added to the growing body of research showing brain trauma doesn't have to reach the level of concussion to be of concern.

Of the eighty-five samples, 80 percent—nearly all of whom played sports—showed evidence of CTE, an incurable brain disease whose symptoms include memory loss, depression, and dementia. CTE symptoms can also mimic those seen in Lou Gehrig's disease and Alzheimer's.

Among the group with CTE, fifty were football players, including six high school football players and nine college football players. The study took four years to complete and included subjects between seventeen and ninety-eight years old.

The research provided more evidence that it's not just concussions that parents, coaches, and doctors need to worry about, but total head trauma, including repetitive smaller subconcussive hits. These hits don't result in any immediate symptoms for the athletes and include routine hits such as those experienced by offensive and defensive linemen, who bang heads play after play.

The study increased the anxiety level at NFL and NHL headquarters, as well as at the headquarters of football, hockey, and soccer organizations from the college level down to the youth level.

YOUTH SPORTS NEEDS TO BE THE FOCUS

While brain trauma at the NFL and college levels is certainly serious stuff, as a nation our biggest area of concern shouldn't be adults who choose to play in the NFL (although we need to make sure every NFL player is fully aware of the risks of participation), it should be the college, high school, and youth athletes whose brains are not fully developed and require more care and recovery time from concussions than adults. On the basis of pure numbers alone, high school and youth contact sports should be the focus.

"The immature brain is still developing," says Bailes. "That makes it more susceptible to damage and more likely to suffer repetitive injury."

Here's the scariest issue in a nutshell: Too many high school and youth athletes suffer concussions without their coaches or parents even knowing it. And too many of these young athletes return to action too quickly—risking dangerous outcomes.

Nearly four hundred thousand concussions occurred in high school athletics during the 2008–2009 school year—most of them in football. Many of these are initially undetected. In the last two years, eight kids have died from concussion-based issues, and dozens more have suffered catastrophic brain injuries.

According to a recent study by the Center for Injury Research and Policy at Nationwide Children's Hospital in Columbus, Ohio, 40.5 percent of high school athletes who have suffered concussions return to action prematurely, risking more severe problems. Playing with a concussion can lead to death from second impact syndrome, a condition in which the brain swells, shutting down the brain stem and resulting in respiratory failure.

It's sobering to note that only 42 percent of high schools have athletic trainers and those trainers obviously can't attend all of a given school's athletic events. Additionally, the vast majority of nonschool-related youth sports leagues, including football, conduct their events without any trainers or trained medical personnel in attendance.

Furthermore, coaches and parents are woefully uneducated when it comes to brain injuries. The result is too few concussions are properly identified and the ones that are don't receive the recommended treatment. Education is critical when it comes to concussions because multiple concussions increase both the short-term and long-term risks for young athletes.

"It's one thing when adults choose to play football," says Hruby. "It's another thing when children are playing football. We generally try to protect children in this society. For example, we don't have eight-year-old kids in coal mines. But we allow eight-year-old kids to risk long-term brain damage playing football."

There is some good news: The National Federation of State High School Associations reviewed the latest research on concussions in young people and sent out a revised pamphlet on concussion policies and procedures to state federations at the end of the 2010–2011 school year.

"We're trying to keep this a front-burner issue," says the federation's Bob Colgate. "Kids are still getting in and playing with head injuries."

Even more encouraging, legislation requiring coaches to be educated about concussion detection and proper protocol in dealing with head injuries is spreading around the country.

Recent laws in Texas, Washington, and Oregon have mandated better concussion training and medical services in youth sports. Sadly, the statutes are usually named after young athletes who were recently killed or seriously hurt by football-related brain injuries.

High-profile lawsuits brought against the NFL by former players, which alleged irresponsible handling of concussion-related injuries, increased the general public's awareness of the problem of concussions in sports—at all levels.

Nevertheless, the vast majority of coaches, parents, and young athletes in this country still aren't fully aware of the seriousness of brain injuries.

"I keep telling kids, your brain is not your knee. It's not your shoulder. It's your future," says neuropsychologist Gerard Gioia. "We have to protect it better than we are."

We'll never be able to eliminate concussions from sports. And it's not feasible or rational to try to keep our sons and daughters in a sports safety bubble. But it's definitely possible to increase the awareness and education levels of all stakeholders in high school and youth sports and to greatly reduce the incidents of concussions, as well as cases of athletes returning to play too soon, which can lead to second impact syndrome and other long-term complications.

"We need to annually educate coaches, parents, and athletes," says Nowinski. "Every athlete needs to know that you don't mess with brain injuries. Almost every athlete knows you don't mess with neck injuries because you can end up paralyzed. In a similar way, every athlete needs to learn about brain trauma and realize you don't take chances with brain injuries. We need to start educating young athletes when they're six years old. We have to get to the point where athletes can recognize the symptoms of concussion in themselves *and* their teammates."

CAN HELMETS HELP?

An important question is how much can we actually protect our brains in sports, especially football? Intuitively, we believe helmets make sports safer, and we think headgear with additional, or more high tech, padding would be even more protective. However, there's a lot of debate in the scientific community these days regarding just how protective helmets can be in regard to brain trauma.

It's important to note that no helmet can prevent concussions.

When it comes to brain injuries, the problem isn't just the initial blow to the head but also the brain's movement inside the skull during collisions. In terms of the brain's movement inside the skull after a blow to the head, the type of padding, or amount of padding, probably doesn't matter very much.

Basically, helmets are of little or no help when it comes to brain injuries. They're great at preventing skull fractures and lacerations but terrible at preventing brain damage. That's because the brain is like Jell-O bouncing up against the walls of the skull. It's the whiplash effect that leads to concussions. That's why players can receive concussions without even being hit in the head. A blow to the chest can send the brain splashing against the skull with as much force as a head-to-head shot.

"The brain is still moving around within the skull when somebody has a concussion, and that's what causes them," said Dr. Mark Lovell, cocreator of the ImPACT concussion test. "We can't put a helmet directly on the brain."

Most current studies in the area of concussions focus on linear impact, i.e., direct helmet-to-helmet contact. However, some neurologists think rotational impact—from a glancing blow that twists the head—is just as dangerous. There are questions about just how much helmets can protect against rotational impact. Some researchers even believe that helmets may increase rotational impact and torque due to their added weight.

Other researchers suggest that big hits aren't the main concussion cause. They say many concussions result from the accumulated damage of lots of minor hits. In that case, helmets may have limited positive impact as well. It's important to consider that the average high school football lineman receives a thousand or more shots to the head during a single football season, based on estimates by Boston University researchers.

Another issue related to helmets is whether or not football helmet manufacturers are being ethical when it comes to marketing their helmets. One such company, Riddell, has claimed its Revolution helmet reduces the risk of concussions by 31 percent versus traditional helmets. However, Senator Tom Udall, D-New Mexico, believes marketing statements such as these are misleading. He went public with his concerns. Following Udall's comments, Riddell said that while its research on reducing concussions was encouraging, "we can't stress enough that no helmet will prevent all concussions."

Along these same lines, the Federal Trade Commission (FTC) is examining the marketing practices of Riddell and other leading manufacturers of football helmets. Their investigation is focused on the companies' claims that football helmets reduce concussions. The FTC agreed to do the investigation at Udall's urging. Udall argued the helmet manufacturers were using "deceptive practices."

"I am concerned for our young football players and their safety," said Udall. "I hope football helmet makers improve their products to address concussion risks. It is simply unacceptable for sports equipment companies to falsely advertise their products to athletes, coaches, and parents with claims of providing a level of safety that does not yet exist."

In soccer there has been a movement—driven primarily by parents—for players to wear headgear to protect the brain in several ways: during collisions between players, when a player's head hits the ground, and also from repetitive headers. A couple of manufacturers have developed protective headgear for soccer players. Some have claimed the new-style headgear significantly reduces the concussion risk. However, the claims are questionable given the lack of hard scientific data on the safety effects of the headgear.

In fact, some researchers believe the soccer headgear actually increases the risk of concussions because the added weight on the head adds stress to the neck and increases the whiplash effect and possibly the rotational impact.

Ultimately, there may be too much emphasis on headgear and not enough on coaching technique when it comes to concussion prevention. There's a widespread belief that coaching reforms and stricter officiating will do more to lower concussion incidence than any style of helmet.

More football coaches, for example, should use the head-up "see what you hit" approach to teaching tackling and blocking because in general head-up hits are less dangerous than head-down hits (spearing). Officials at all levels of football need to make mitigating helmet-to-helmet hits an officiating "point of emphasis" in order to help change player behavior.

"The best results for concussion reduction will come from changing football behavior," says Guskiewicz.

Nevertheless, the big question remains, can football be made safe enough—especially for young participants—without completely changing the essence of the game?

RECOMMENDATIONS

We're not anti-sports, we're pro-children. We're not attacking sports, we're defending the brains of kids who don't know any better, who will ram their head into anything.

We should definitely still play sports. There are many redeeming qualities to sports. But there's zero redeeming qualities to head trauma. We have a culture that's very accepting of brain trauma and that needs to change. It needs to be unacceptable to put kids in sports where we're encouraging them getting hit in the head.

> Chris Nowinski, codirector of the Center for the Study of Traumatic Encephalopathy at Boston University

I. All Sports Leagues—at All Levels—Should Be Required to Develop a Concussion Policy and Implement an Educational Campaign on Brain Trauma

Sports leagues—from the little leagues to the big leagues—should develop concussion policy statements that include the league's commitment to safety; a description of concussion and repetitive brain trauma, including signs and symptoms of concussion; the process in place if an athlete is suspected of having a concussion; and information on when athletes can safely return to play.

A well-conceived concussion policy is important at all levels of sports, but is especially critical at the high school and youth levels because younger brains take longer to heal from a concussion and are more susceptible to second impact syndrome.

Part of every league's concussion policy should be a section spelling out the education and communications strategy for increasing stakeholder awareness and understanding of brain injuries.

Parents, coaches, trainers, and athletes should be asked to sign the concussion policy statement at the beginning of each sports season—in conjunction with mandatory attendance at a brain trauma seminar.

"I tell youth sports parents to get educated and try to make an informed decision," says Nowinski. "Nobody should expose kids to repetitive brain trauma without knowledge of what the potential ramifications could be."

The most critical aspect of a concussion safety plan is the quick identification of a possible concussion during games and practices.

The King-Devick test is a simple and objective rapid sideline-screening test for concussions that can be administered by coaches, trainers, and parents in two minutes or less. Some sports medicine professionals have called the test "the missing link" in concussion safety protocols. Every sports league from high school down should seriously consider making the King-Devick test part of its concussion policy and concussion management protocol.

Research has shown the King-Devick test to be an accurate and reliable method of identifying athletes with brain injuries. It can be an excellent objective tool for determining whether players should be removed from games or not.

A University of Pennsylvania School of Medicine study published in the Journal of Neurology on April 26, 2011, demonstrated the usefulness of the King-Devick test. The study examined thirty-nine boxers and mixed martial arts contestants and found post-fight test times for those who suffered head trauma worsened by an average 11.1 seconds. Those who had lost consciousness were on average eighteen seconds slower. Those who did not suffer any head trauma actually improved their times by more than a second on average.

"This rapid screening test provides an effective way to detect early signs of concussion, which can improve outcomes and hopefully prevent repetitive concussions," said Laura Balcer, the study's senior researcher.

The King-Devick test is a one-time, one- to two-minute test that requires an athlete to establish a baseline time at the beginning of each season. Athletes are timed reading a series of single-digit numbers displayed on three flash cards. If the athlete suffers a suspected head injury in a practice or game, the athlete is given the test again. If the time needed to complete the test is more than five seconds slower than the athlete's baseline test, a concussion can be confidently diagnosed. The athlete should then be removed from play and evaluated by a licensed medical professional.

There are other concussion tests available. However, they are more complex and should be administered by professional health-care providers. The King-Devick test is easy to learn, understand, and administer by any adult, making it very valuable for high school and youth sports programs.

Signs and Symptoms of Concussion
Appears dazed or stunned
Forgets plays
Unsure of score or opponent
Moves clumsily (balance problems)
Loses consciousness (even briefly)
Headache or pressure in the head
Nausea or vomiting
Double or blurry vision
Sensitivity to light or noise
Feels groggy or sluggish

2. Every State Should Adopt Concussion Legislation Similar to Colorado's Jake Snakenberg Youth Concussion Act

The Colorado youth sports concussion act is named for Jake Snakenberg, a football player at Grandview High School in Aurora, Colorado, who died in 2004 as a result of second impact syndrome.

Briefly this legislation entails the following:

- Requires coaches who suspect an athlete has a concussion to immediately remove that athlete from play for the remainder of the game or practice.
- In order for the athlete to return to play, written clearance from a licensed health-care provider is needed.
- All coaches of athletes ranging in age from eleven to nineteen are required to take a free thirty-minute online concussion course that teaches them to recognize concussion symptoms.

At its most basic, the policy can be summarized as "When in doubt, sit them out."

"This would've meant a lot to Jake, and he would be very proud, just as we are, that his name is associated with keeping kids safe. . . . No family should ever have to go through what my family has been through," said Snakenberg's mother, Kelli Jantz.

One strong addition to this type of legislation would be to make the entire team take the concussion course so players would be more apt to see signs of concussion in their teammates. In many cases, teammates can see the signs of concussion before coaches do.

The Snakenberg Act has been endorsed by the NFL (which, after years of resisting the research on concussions and attempting to sweep it under the rug, is finally—albeit gradually and reluctantly—acknowledging that improved awareness, prevention, and treatment measures are needed). The number of states with similar laws on the books is growing. The goal needs to be a law of this type in all fifty states.

Former Denver Broncos receiver Ed McCaffrey personally endorsed the Colorado bill, saying, "We know way more today than we did when I played and it is important that we take advantage of that knowledge."

3. Ban Football in Public Middle Schools and High Schools

> When it comes to football, society's going to have to make a lot of big decisions in the coming years.
>
> Patrick Hruby, sports and culture writer

Given the immense popularity of football in this country, this likely will be the most controversial recommendation in this book.

Across the United States, there are approximately 1.3 million high school football players.

UNIVERSITY OF WINCHESTER
LIBRARY

It's important to note that football, alone among high school sports, is inherently unsafe for the brain. Football is the one high school sport in which a primary objective is inflicting physical punishment on one's opponent. (Boxing is rarely offered at the high school level.) Unlike other sports, you can't make football significantly safer for the brain without changing the nature of the game (e.g., banning blocking and tackling).

Our public high schools—created to develop students' brains—shouldn't be sponsoring an activity that is clearly a significant threat to players' brains. An increasing amount of research makes it clear that football is too dangerous for the human brain, especially young, still-developing brains. It's hazardous to one's health, just like smoking.

Once the evidence on smoking was clear, we banned it from our high school campuses. The same fate should now happen to football.

What about new safety measures? There simply aren't enough safety measures we can implement to overcome the fact that the brain isn't built to withstand the repetitive brain trauma inherent in a game built around violent collisions.

As noted earlier, helmets are of little or no help when it comes to preventing brain damage due to the whiplash effect on the brain that leads to concussions.

According to the Brain Injury Research Institute, in any given season, 20 percent of high school football players sustain brain injuries. That number should be unacceptable to parents, school administrators, and school board members.

Clearly, football has a serious problem here. And there's no fix unless we eliminate blocking and tackling and go to flag football at the high school level.

Undeniably, the demise of high school football will be a culture shock for schools and communities around the country. Culture-change experts say it takes seven years to fully adapt to major change. But using taxpayer dollars to fund a school activity that is clearly detrimental to the brain simply isn't justifiable.

Football proponents will argue that the game imparts lessons on the gridiron that can't be learned anywhere else. But life lessons like teamwork, leadership, perseverance, sacrifice, goal setting, discipline, etc., can be just as easily and effectively acquired by participating in sports other than football.

"I ask people all the time, 'Would you want your child involved with a junior high or high school boxing or MMA [mixed martial arts] team?'" says Hruby. "In terms of the dangers of brain trauma, there's very little difference between those two sports and football."

Football at the high school level is doomed. It's just a matter of time. If parents don't rise up to stop it—in a Mothers Against Drunk Driving mode—insurance companies will. Inevitably, the new brain research will lead to lawsuits at all levels of the game, including high school football. Football-related risk and liability will be hard to contain. And, when risk and liability can't be contained, insurance premium costs will shoot up, making football sponsorship cost prohibitive for high schools.

Banning high school football doesn't mean youth football will be dead. There will still be private club football organizations available for kids (and their parents) who want to continue pursuing football. The call here isn't to ban all youth football in the United States, just the public funding of football in our public schools.

Opponents may cry "Overcautiousness!" However, we're talking about brains here, not knees, ankles, and shoulders. As Jeffrey Kluger wrote in a January 31, 2011, *Time* article titled "Headbanger Nation": "Athletics will never be stripped of all danger . . . but the brain is more than a joint or a limb. It's the seat of the self. We overlook that fact at our peril and—much worse—at our children's."

It may be ten years, twenty years, or thirty years before middle school and high school football's gone, but it will be gone. We can't put the medical research we're now aware of back in the bottle. But why do we have to wait? Let's act now and spare numerous young athletes—and their families—from dealing with the tragedies associated with football-induced brain trauma.

4. Work to Make All Sports as "Brain Safe" as Possible

> We need to fully recognize what the brain can handle and structure our sports from that knowledge. Every aspect of each sport should be reconsidered with an eye towards brain trauma.
>
> Chris Nowinski, author of *Head Games: Football's Concussion Crisis*

A 2009–2010 study of high school athletes found concussions to be a significant issue in the following sports: football, hockey, boys' lacrosse, girls' soccer, girls' lacrosse, wrestling, boys' soccer, girls' basketball, and boys' basketball.

Given what we now know regarding brain trauma in sports, high school and youth sports policy makers in these sports—and others—need to evaluate their sports for brain trauma risks and do what they can to protect the brains of the young athletes participating. (See Sports Legacy Institute's Minimum Recommended Guidelines for Youth Sports on page 52.) This initiative is especially critical for young athletes, whose bodies and brains are still developing.

Dr. Robert Cantu, a specialist on brain trauma in sports, points out that kids are more likely to get a concussion because their heads are a bigger part of their body than an adult's head is and because their necks aren't as strong during their developmental years.

SPORTS LEGACY INSTITUTE'S MINIMUM RECOMMENDED GUIDELINES FOR YOUTH SPORTS

(1) **Preseason education for coaches, parents, and athletes**. Preseason concussion and brain trauma education should be required for coaches, parents, and athletes.

(2) **Youth programs should adopt the CDC *Heads Up* Concussion Action Plan**. If you suspect that a player has a concussion, you should take the following steps:

  a. Remove athlete from play.

  b. Ensure athlete is evaluated by an appropriate health-care professional. Do not try and judge the seriousness of the injury yourself.

  c. Inform athlete's parents or guardians about the known or possible concussion and give them the CDC fact sheet on concussion.

  d. Allow athlete to return to play *only* with permission from an appropriate health-care professional.

(3) **Utilize CDC *Heads Up* stickers on clipboards**. Stickers make for easy access to both a list of common concussive signs and symptoms and an action plan if an athlete potentially experiences a concussion.

(4) **Prevention through neck strengthening**. Studies have shown that neck strength may be an important factor in reducing the forces on the brain resulting from impacts to the head.

(5) **Prevention through overall brain trauma reduction**. Coaches should monitor total brain trauma and strive to reduce both the number of hits to the head that players receive and the severity. This includes activities like blocking and tackling in football and headers in soccer.

Repetitive brain trauma suffered in youth sports is believed to lead to some athletes developing the progressive neurodegenerative brain disease CTE, which can eventually lead to dementia. CTE may be more correlated to total lifetime brain trauma than concussions.

IT'S TIME TO TAKE ADULT EGOS OUT OF YOUTH SPORTS

In too many cases today, adults—driven by ego and avarice—are warping the original intent of youth sports. Children as young as nine and ten years old are being forced to specialize in a single sport by coaches and parents with stars and/or dollar signs in their eyes. In the quest for that elusive athletic scholarship, Olympic team berth, or even a pro sports career, our children are being turned into mini-professionals who, when not training with their competitive club team, are being dragged to a personal trainer or some elite camp or tournament. The results too often aren't pretty: emotional burnout, overuse injuries, and kids dropping out of sports by age thirteen because the fun is gone.

Ralph Nader, founder, League of Fans

We all need to think more deeply about the insanity of our youth sports culture, with its focus on early specialization in one sport, and, especially, its seasons without end.

Michael Sokolove, author of *Warrior Girls*

Youth sports: a chance to run around, play sports with friends, and have fun. At least that's how it used to be.

Today, our kids' sports have been hijacked by adults who professionalize them and attempt to meet their own needs through youth sports. For the most part, these parents and coaches usually have good intentions but the damage to our young people is real nonetheless.

Sometimes parents want that magical athletic scholarship more than their child does. They'd like to be able to tell the people in their lives that their kid got a full-ride athletic scholarship to State U. Others are trying to live out their athletic dreams through their children. It's called achievement-by-proxy syndrome.

"A lot of parents have a belief that says, 'How well my kid does on the field reflects on me as a parent,'" says Jim Thompson, founder of the Positive Coaching Alliance. "One of my mentors, John Gardner, once said, 'The toughest thing kids have to face is the unfulfilled lives of their parents.' I think there's a lot of truth in that."

For other parents, youth sports provide the centerpiece of their entertainment and social life. And then there are a growing number of profit-seeking adults in the youth sports field—club sports administrators, personal trainers and coaches, tournament and camp organizers—who are all too willing to make a buck off parents' dreams of athletic glory for their children.

As a whole, our youth sports system is broken. As our performance culture increasingly focuses on the development of elite athletes at the youth sports level (in many cases, at the expense of a "sports for all" philosophy that would significantly help address our country's childhood obesity epidemic; see chapter 6, "Physical Education and Sports for All Students"), our kids are burning out emotionally at a greater clip and at an earlier age.

Research shows that nearly 80 percent of all children who play adult-organized youth sports drop out by the time they're thirteen. The reason most often cited is that it's no longer fun. The primary reason it's no longer fun? Overzealous adults, in the form of parents and/or coaches.

And our kids' bodies are breaking down with overuse injuries at an alarming rate.

"With specialization, the danger is that kids use the same muscle groups, day in and day out, and this wears out the muscles," says Michael Sokolove, author of *Warrior Girls*.

Fred Bowen is the author of eighteen books for kids that combine sports fiction and sports history. He also writes a weekly sports column for kids in the *Washington Post*. He agrees with Sokolove regarding the dangerous adult-driven trend toward more and more specialization in youth sports.

"I think you can see overbearing adults in all the youth sports issues today. For example, let's take specialization, playing only one sport at a young age. I had the privilege of interviewing Cal Ripken one time and I asked him when was the first time he played baseball year-round. He told me, 'When I signed a professional contract at eighteen.'

"I point out to parents that Ripken was an all-state soccer player in high school. Ripken was a big man for a shortstop but he could really move his feet. Soccer helped him with his footwork. San Francisco 49ers quarterback Colin Kaepernick was not only a standout football player in high school, he was also an excellent basketball player. But people who saw him a lot in high school said his best sport was probably baseball.

"The American Academy of Pediatrics specifically says don't specialize in youth sports. So, if kids specialize by focusing on playing a single sport year-round, they are doing so against doctors' orders. And adults who allow specialization, or encourage it, are going against doctors' orders as well."

Why is this happening? What's going on?

Ego is a factor. Too many parents are living the "athletic scholarship/pro athlete dream" for themselves, pushing their kids too hard, and in the process taking the passion and joy out of sports.

And good old human greed plays a role as well. There are a growing number of profit-driven adults in the youth sports field—club sports administrators, personal trainers and coaches, tournament and camp organizers—who are all too willing to sell the full-ride scholarship dream to parents (who are either gullible, uninformed, or ego-driven—sometimes a little of all three—when it comes to the possibility of an athletic scholarship for their son or daughter) in order to make a buck. These youth sports vultures are increasingly leveraging the dreams of youngsters and their parents for their own financial benefit. It doesn't matter how athletically challenged some of these kids are, the sales pitch from these youth sports entrepreneurs remains the same whether it's delivered implicitly or explicitly: "If you come work with me/us for $XXX a week, I can get you that scholarship."

"We have people making a living from youth sports," says Thompson. "There are basketball and soccer trainers who will benefit financially if you go to their camps, training sessions, and play on their spring and fall teams.

"Jay Coakley [a leading sports sociologist] believes youth sport is child labor revisited. You have entrepreneurs making money in youth sports, and the staff, in a sense, is made up of young kids. That's a problem."

Another unfortunate side effect of our high-pressure performance sports culture is that as a society we are inadvertently dividing the youth sports landscape into the "haves" and "have-nots," as lower-income kids are being left behind, unable to afford club fees and the cost of personal trainers, coaches, and camps.

"It's the trickle-down of the professionalization of pro and college sports—all the way down to the youth level," says sports and politics journalist Dave Zirin. "The cost of youth sports is getting out of reach for the average family. There's a good book by Mark Hyman about this subject called *The Most Expensive Game in Town*. It's a look at the economics of youth sports.

"By high school, we're sectioning kids off, we're identifying 'future pros' at an early age. We have to get better at getting out the message that there's a place in sports for everybody. Not everyone can find a place in the pros but participating in sports is still valuable for all of us."

ACHIEVEMENT-BY-PROXY SYNDROME

Dr. Chris Stankovich, a sport psychology consultant and advocate for positive youth sports development, does a nice job summarizing the issues involved with a key youth sports issue today: burnout.

> Youth sports burnout in America is increasing at an alarming rate, and millions of kids nationwide are becoming both mentally and physically fatigued from playing sports too intensely, often year-round. Sadly, this phenomenon seems to be getting worse, and not better. This is probably due in large part to several contributing factors: Our country's great love of sports; increasing numbers of families turning to sports as a means of a free college education (or even an opportunity at professional sports); and parents living vicariously through their children and holding on to the pluralistic ignorant notion that "more is better" in terms of their kids playing sports better than they themselves did as kids. In response to our hunger in America to create more youth sport opportunities to meet those needs and expectations, a perfect storm has evolved—youth sport leagues starting at earlier ages, premier/travel teams in every community, and year-round specialization camps and clinics seemingly everywhere so that kids can become masters of their respective sports—and in half the time it took their parents.

The issue of coaches and parents obsessing about high school varsity status, all-league and all-state teams, scholarships, and pro contracts has become so commonplace that psychiatrists have dubbed the condition achievement-by-proxy syndrome—adults living vicariously through the exploits of their children.

Of course the issue of overbearing parents and coaches in youth sports isn't a new one. However, things are definitely getting worse. Adults are taking their seriousness about youth sports to new, unhealthy extremes. The number of incidents of physical violence and verbal abuse at youth sporting events has increased significantly over the last decade. According to the National Alliance for Youth Sports, approximately 15 percent of youth sports games played today involve a confrontation between parents, between parents and officials, between parents and coaches, or between coaches and officials. That's a jump from 5 percent a decade ago.

CHANCES OF PLAYING COLLEGE OR PRO SPORTS ARE SLIM

Simply put, when it comes to youth sports, as parents and coaches—as *adults*—we need to chill out. Our sons and daughters almost assuredly aren't going to be pro athletes. Statisticians believe you have a better chance of being murdered than becoming a professional athlete. And it's extremely unlikely our children will receive a college athletic scholarship. Only 1 to 2 percent of high school senior athletes get a college athletic scholarship—partial or full. The percentage of high school senior athletes receiving "full-ride" athletic scholarships (which cover tuition, books, and room and board) is well under 1 percent.

"The more we can educate parents to have a realistic idea of what they're trying to accomplish when they put their kid in youth sports—and the more we can help them be more realistic about things like college athletic scholarships—the better it will be for the kids, and the more fun they'll have," says Bowen.

It's time for a serious reality check for everyone involved. NCAA research reveals the odds of becoming a college or pro athlete are steep:

Men's Basketball

- High school senior basketball players who go on to play NCAA men's basketball (all divisions— I, II, and III, including walk-ons): less than one in thirty-five, or 2.9 percent.
- NCAA seniors drafted by an NBA team: less than one in seventy-five, or 1.3 percent.
- High school seniors eventually drafted by an NBA team: about three in ten thousand, or 0.03 percent.

Women's Basketball

- High school senior basketball players who go on to play NCAA women's basketball (all divisions): about three in one hundred, or 3.1 percent.

- NCAA seniors drafted by a WNBA team: about one in one hundred, or 1 percent.
- High school seniors eventually drafted by a WNBA team: about one in five thousand, or 0.02 percent.

Football

- High school senior football players who go on to play NCAA football (all divisions): about one in seventeen, or 5.8 percent.
- NCAA seniors drafted by an NFL team: about one in fifty, or 2 percent.
- High school seniors eventually drafted by an NFL team: about nine in ten thousand, or 0.09 percent.

Baseball

- High school senior baseball players who go on to play NCAA baseball (all divisions): less than three in fifty, or 5.6 percent.
- NCAA seniors drafted by an MLB team: less than eleven in one hundred, or 10.5 percent.
- High school seniors eventually drafted by an MLB team: about one in two hundred, or 0.5 percent. (However, these players almost always go to the minor leagues, where the odds of making it to the majors remain steep.)

For a bigger wake-up call—for young athletes and their parents and coaches—consider that the numbers above for professional sports leagues refer to those *drafted* by a pro sports franchise. Actually making a big-league roster and playing in a professional game at the highest level is even tougher.

Rest assured, the odds are similar for Major League Soccer (MLS), tennis, golf, and other professional sports not listed above.

The takeaway: Go ahead and dream big but keep things in perspective.

PARENTING AND COACHING STYLES ARE CRITICAL

Regardless of a kid's athletic ability, adults who drive their kids too hard in sports—and too early—have a much greater chance of seeing these kids burn out and quit before they finish high school than they do seeing them receive athletic scholarships.

So let's relax, and more importantly, let our kids relax. Then we'll start to see the dropout rate start to decline.

Today, by the time most young athletes reach the age of twelve they've been involved in some type of adult-organized youth sport for seven or eight years. They've witnessed numerous incidents of "grown-ups" yelling at players, officials, and coaches. They've probably experienced several grueling postgame critiques of their play by Coach, Mom, or Dad. They've survived many seasons of adults screaming at them to "stay in position," "get back on defense," and "be more aggressive." It's quite possible they've been encouraged by "well-meaning" adults to specialize in a single sport in order to increase their chances of making the high school varsity team or landing a college scholarship.

Sadly, this weekend, all over the United States, young children will wake up with a sense of dread in their stomachs because they fear Mom and/or Dad's intense scrutiny at their game that day. When kids see how important their games are to their parents they get anxious.

To a lot of young athletes, sports just aren't games to play, they're vehicles by which they gain or lose the affection of their parents, the most important people in their lives. What began as fun is now a pressure-filled exercise. Children are always seeking a sense of unconditional love from their parents, and when it comes to sports participation they seldom get it.

And when these youngsters go off to practice, they often have to deal with a coach who's more drill sergeant than educator. That's nonsense. Young athletes, whether they're eight or eighteen, shouldn't have to endure boot camp in order to play the sport they love.

"I think there are certainly limits to the military approach to coaching—and those limits are even lower when it comes to youth sports," says legendary sportswriter Frank Deford. "Just because you can say and do certain things to grown-ups in this society doesn't give you the license to be able to say and do those things to children simply because you happen to be a football coach."

MAKING SPORTS FUN IS THE KEY TO SUCCESS

Get this: Despite what your high school coach might've told you, having fun at practice or during a game doesn't hinder your chances of success—it's the key to it!

You may think that if you perform well, you'll be happy and have fun. But research says you should flip that around. In other words, if you learn to have fun and be happy while competing, you'll perform better and have more success on the scoreboard. Studies show that athletes who focus on having fun versus performing well are more relaxed, creative, and "in the zone" more often. In short, they enjoy sports more and, as a bonus, perform better.

Helping to ensure that sports remain fun for kids is also the best way to enhance the chances of long-term success. If adults make sports fun for kids, there's a good chance they'll develop a passion for the game. When that happens, they'll be intrinsically motivated to succeed and they won't need coaches or parents constantly pushing them and dragging them to practice. As sociologist Alfie Kohn notes, "Nothing, according to the research, predicts excellence like finding the task fun."

My favorite example of a coach who followed this philosophy is John Gagliardi, the former football coach at Division III Saint John's University in Minnesota. Gagliardi is the winningest coach in college football history. In 2003 he won his fourth national championship, to go along with thirty conference titles. In sixty-three years as a college head coach, his record was 489-138-11. Gagliardi didn't carry a whistle. He didn't berate players. He had no film sessions after Monday, no tackling in practice, no playbooks, no blocking sleds, and no wind sprints. Nobody got cut. His players laughingly mocked traditional military-style calisthenics at the beginning of practices—which were limited to ninety minutes. Players loved coming to practice and Gagliardi's graduation record was nearly perfect.

What makes Gagliardi and his methods so interesting is the fact that his approach is such an exception to the norm in SportsWorld.

YOUTH SPORTS ARE FINE IF YOU MINIMIZE THE INFLUENCE OF ADULT EGOS

> Change is always going to come relatively slowly on things that are so sewn into our culture. The only way things will change in youth sports is if enough parents decide they're going to use another model. Things will change in youth sports when parents begin to focus on the well-being of their kids.
>
> Jay Coakley, sports sociologist, author of *Sports in Society*

There's nothing inherently wrong with adult-organized youth sports. They can be the source of wonderful, healthy, and happy experiences for children—*if* adults can balance their desire to win (and, in some cases, their desire to make money off of kids' love of sports) with the holistic development of kids and having fun. Striving to win has never been the problem;

it's the win-at-all-cost (WAAC)—and in some cases the profit-at-all-cost (PAAC) mentality—that is the problem.

Youth sports, driven by WAAC and PAAC mentalities, is, in actuality, youth sports abuse.

"In many ways, there's no more important issue than changing the youth sports culture," says Thompson. "Transforming youth sports can positively impact our country in many ways. How youth sports are conducted infiltrates our collective mind-set."

Adults who are pathologically focused on winning plague virtually every youth sports league and event. Yes, the majority of parents and coaches do a pretty good job of keeping youth sports in perspective but it only takes a handful of adults—especially coaches—to ruin the sports experience for a bunch of kids.

"I think the excessive focus on winning is so destructive in sports—at all levels—but especially in youth sports," says former Wheelock College athletic director and longtime sports administrator Diana Cutaia. "This winning obsession is created by adults and transferred to our kids. It takes away the joy of sports from kids. Kids need that joy in their lives to function optimally.

"The emphasis on winning in sports negatively impacts how you deal with both teammates and opponents. It becomes about 'How much better can I be than you?' and 'How badly can I beat you?' It's not about collaboration, helping the person next to you. For coaches and players, it becomes about a 'power-over' model, how much power can I have over someone else?"

One area that needs to be monitored—and in some cases regulated—is "youth sports entrepreneurs." An increasing number of club sports administrators, personal trainers, instructors, tournament organizers, and camp directors are using the dream of college athletic scholarships and professional careers to pull money out of the wallets of ill-informed and starry-eyed parents of young athletes. To that end, they're doing things like scheduling soccer tournaments in oppressive July heat and humidity and putting kids' health at risk.

Seldom is the question "What's best for the kids?" asked by these folks.

Youth sports parents and coaches need to focus less on winning (and in some cases making money) and more on sports as a vehicle to build teamwork and leadership abilities, improve sports skills, enhance fitness, promote healthy lifestyles, gain experiences that teach lifetime lessons and shape values, develop friendships—some for a lifetime—and have fun (what surveys show kids want most from sports participation).

"Listen, most kids who play rec sports aren't going to play high school," says Bowen. "Most kids who play high school aren't going to play college. And almost nobody plays pros. But everyone is going to be a citizen, and if we're not teaching young people how to be better citizens through sports then we're pretty much missing the boat with youth sports."

RECOMMENDATIONS

> Youth sports, indeed, is the most important institution in all sports.
>
> Tom Farrey, ESPN investigative reporter,
youth sports reformer, and author

Unquestionably, when youth sports are operated to meet the needs and desires of adults, kids get hurt emotionally and physically.

How do we turn it around? What should our goals be for youth sports?

In Tom Farrey's excellent book on youth sports, *Game On: How the Pressure to Win at All Costs Endangers Youth Sports and What Parents Can Do about It*, former General Electric CEO Jack Welch suggested the "valuable and important challenge" for youth sports was to achieve the trifecta of (1) excellence; (2) character development; and (3) broad-based participation.

That three-part objective sounds fine as long as "excellence" means focusing on intrinsic measures (giving your best effort, competing against one's potential, maximizing the gifts one has), and not just extrinsic measures (e.g., winning medals, team championships, or scholarships).

In regard to Welch's reference to "character development," use of that term can have some volatile consequences. It means different things to different people, and in some people's eyes it has religious connotations. However, if by "character development" Welch means things like developing the whole child, stressing effort, attitude, and sportsmanship in competition, learning from mistakes, and spending some time developing things like leadership and teamwork skills, then he's right on track.

In terms of Welch's third objective for youth sports, broad-based participation, I couldn't agree more. In an era of a childhood obesity epidemic, it's critical to increase sports participation in youth sports.

With this general vision for youth sports in mind, the following six-part plan has been developed to enhance the positives of youth sports and mitigate the negatives.

1. Put the Phrase "The Needs of the Kids Come First" in Every Youth Sports Organization's Mission Statement

Effectively addressing the youth sports problem in this country requires a multifaceted solution, but the starting point must be looking for ways to put the *youth* back in youth sports. This will require implementing measures designed to limit the influence of adult egos in our kids' games. The mantra "put the needs of kids first" should drive all policy making and decision making within every youth sports organization.

2. Implement a National Youth Sports Coaching Education Program

A youth sports coaching education program is sorely needed in this country. Youth sports coaches spend hundreds of hours with our children. In many cases, they have more face-to-face time with our kids than classroom teachers do. Yet public school teachers have to go through an extensive education and certification process, while youth sports coaches can basically just show up with a whistle and clipboard and be considered qualified. In addition to sport knowledge, youth coaches need to have knowledge about effective teaching methodologies and child development approaches, as well as safety and injury-prevention measures.

The National Association for Sport and Physical Education recommends that all coaches be required to complete coach education training commensurate with the level of competition prior to working with athletes. Specifically they recommend:

- Developing an infrastructure to track and record the number of coaches who have completed coaching education programs.
- Developing recruitment and selection procedures that identify persons with high moral character and integrity for coaching positions.
- Providing and utilizing positive incentives to encourage completion of coaching education requirements.

Given the problems with youth sports in this country, along with the growing childhood obesity epidemic we're facing, it's the youth sports sector of SportsWorld that should be getting favorable treatment from the government, not wealthy pro sports owners or big-time college athletics programs. Part of that favorable treatment should include funding for a national education program for youth sports coaches. The goal should be to get all youth sports coaches through the program.

Currently our governmental institutions give all kinds of economic advantages to pro sports entities, including antitrust exemptions at the national level and tax subsidies and sweetheart leases for stadiums at the state and local levels. Moreover, highly commercialized big-time college sports departments operate with a tax-exempt status bestowed by our government.

From a policy perspective, it's time we turned this around and put more emphasis on developing positive youth sports experiences (for all children, not just the athletically inclined) in this country.

3. Enforce the Ted Stevens Sports Act

The Ted Stevens Sports Act calls for the promotion of broad-based sports participation by the United States Olympic Committee (USOC) and National Governing Bodies (NGBs) for each sport. Currently, however, these groups focus almost exclusively on the development of elite athletes. The spirit of the Sports Act is that no child athlete should be left behind (no athlete of any age for that matter). Nevertheless, the reality is that broad-based participation is an afterthought for the USOC and NGBs. That needs to change.

4. Demand Public Schools Prioritize Physical Education and Broad-Based Sports Participation Instead of Varsity Programs

> By puberty, most American children have been classified as failed athletes and assigned to watch and cheer for those who have survived the first of several major "cuts."
>
> Robert Lipsyte, sports journalist

Our schools are supposed to be in the business of education, not creating elite sports teams. If club sports organizations outside our school system want to focus on developing elite athletes and top-level sports teams, that is their prerogative (although they should be encouraged to offer sports opportunities for all levels of athletic ability, as the European club sports model does).

State legislators and public school policy makers should be pushed to develop school policies that increase physical education and intramural sports opportunities. Less focus should be on varsity programs that only serve a small percentage of the student body. This doesn't mean varsity athletics programs need to be eliminated (except football; see chapter 3, "Concussion Research Demands New Policies"). They still can have their place and serve a positive purpose. Quality physical education and intramural sports programs can coexist with varsity athletics, but PE and intramural sports should be the first priorities.

Educators should be promoting lifetime physical activity and sports participation for all students based on current research that clearly shows exercise and physical fitness enhances wellness, improves learning readiness, and decreases behavioral problems (see chapter 6, "Physical Education and Sports for All Students").

5. Develop a Broad-Based Communications Campaign Discouraging Early Specialization in a Single Sport

> There's an assumption that specialization makes kids better at their sport, that it promotes mastery. But it doesn't. Every expert will tell you that it absolutely doesn't.
>
> Michael Sokolove, author *Warrior Girls*

Thousands of our young people are now specializing in a single sport by the time they reach the age of ten. Many more are specializing by the age of twelve—before puberty kicks in for a lot of them. There are many documented dangers of early specialization, including emotional and physical burnout and an increased risk of overuse injuries.

In recent years, overuse injuries have quadrupled, and half of all pediatric sports injuries are linked to burnout. The American Academy of Orthopedic Surgeons reports that overuse injuries account for nearly half of all injuries sustained by middle school and high school athletes. Moreover, the American College of Sports Medicine estimates that half of such overuse injuries are preventable.

The American Academy of Pediatrics has said the goal of youth participation in sports "should be to promote lifelong physical activity, recreation and skills of healthy competition"—not to obtain a college scholarship or to make an Olympic or professional team.

Additionally, the National Athletic Trainers' Association recently issued a position paper with a list of recommendations for protecting the health of our young athletes. It recommended that "children take time off between sports seasons and, if they do participate in a single sport year-round, that they take breaks from the sport of two or three nonconsecutive months each year."

Besides the overuse injury risks, early specialization and year-round participation in one sport becomes tedious for kids and the fun level falls. As a result, the dropout rate is higher than it should be.

"Very few kids want to do the same thing, day after day, month after month, because it's not fun," says Sokolove. "Playing different sports is what kids are meant to do. But the culture of youth sports demands that they play one sport only." It's that culture that needs to be changed.

6. Focus on Fun and Utilize the Sports Enjoyment Scorecard

Having fun should also be added to Jack Welch's trifecta of objectives for youth sports mentioned earlier, for several reasons: (1) surveys show fun is the number one reason kids play sports; (2) finding sports no longer fun is the number one reason kids drop out of sports; and (3) research shows that "having fun" predicts better performance.

Why do you play sports? Why do you watch sports?

When you ask both kids and adults these questions, the answer is usually some variation of "It's fun!"

Yet if a visitor from another galaxy watched how we act on our sporting fields, courts, and golf courses, that visitor would never guess we were partaking in sports for fun. Imagine what our celestial guest might witness . . .

- Angry youth sports parents yelling at volunteer coaches, teenage game officials, and, worst of all, screaming at their own kids for not playing better or doing what they—enlightened sports gurus that they are— would do if they were in those tiny ten-year-old bodies.
- Kids who are pouting more than smiling during games, whether it's because they got benched, made a mistake, or were yelled at by their coach (as if they were multimillion-dollar Major Leaguers who just botched a cutoff play).
- Double-digit handicap golfers out on the golf course for "recreation," cursing at themselves, slamming clubs, complaining to their playing partners about the state of their games, and then going home grumpy to unsuspecting spouses and children.
- Fans, who spend thousands of dollars for tickets, parking, concessions, and souvenirs, screaming at the players, coaches, and officials on the field, flipping off fellow fans (or, in some cases, striking them), and turning purple in the face over the poor play of "their" teams.
- Coaches determined to turn play into work, convinced that the only way to help their players perform better is to strut around like drill sergeants instead of being teachers.

You get the idea. We're all too uptight—all in the name of fun!

Okay, I can hear you loud and clear. Sports are the most fun when you or your team is performing well and winning. I get it. Winning is a fun experience. But is that the only reason you're into sports? If so, you're going to be bummed out a lot. In every game, one team wins and one team loses. So, if you're going to make sports a big part of your life you're going to have to figure out a way to deal effectively with losing.

Here are five quick tips to help make your sports experiences more fun—whether you're a young athlete, parent, or coach:

1. **Smile**. Lighten up! It's a game, for Pete's sake, not an economic crisis, health care reform, or conflict in the Middle East. This applies even if you're a pro athlete. Remember Magic Johnson smiling his way to multiple MVPs and NBA titles?

2. **Make your own scoreboard**. Focus on effort, not outcome. Are you (or your youngster) giving your best effort? If so, you're winning. You can't control how well your opponent plays.

3. **Trust your soul, ignore your ego**. Your ego is that voice in your head that screams at you, "You (or your kid) are not measuring up. You're going to make a fool of yourself. You'll be a laughingstock." Your soul is the voice that whispers, "Just relax. Be yourself. You're fine. Whatever happens happens. It's just a game." Turn off the ego. Listen to your soul. Focus on effort over outcomes, as John Wooden, perhaps the greatest team sports coach of all time, did.

4. **No competition, no game**. In sports, it's easy to see the competition as the enemy. But in reality, we're in this together. We all love sports. So, appreciate the other team for helping you get better, pushing you to give your best, and bringing the drama to sports. Play your guts out and then shake hands. Even better, have a postgame drink or snack together. That's a common practice in the highly competitive rugby world. It should become so in all sports.

5. **Remember when and why you fell in love with sports**. Think back, when did you first fall in love with sports? What was it about sports that grabbed you and wouldn't let go? Reflect on your answers a couple times a year (or at least before you go chasing the referee into the parking lot after little Dustin's or Rachel's basketball game).

6. **Think camaraderie, not winning**. The best thing about sports is that they connect people, often for life. Sharing the wins and losses, ups and downs, is what it's all about.

"Almost everyone feels happier when they're with other people," observed sociologist and *Flow* author Mihaly Csikszentmihalyi. "Sports are a great way to be with other people."

In the end, what you'll cherish most about sports—as a player or a fan—are the relationships you've developed through sports. You'll finally realize that the scoreboard you spent so much time focusing on really wasn't that important.

And that realization is the biggest win of all.

THE SPORTS ENJOYMENT SCORECARD

When it comes to sports, we all need to occasionally reset our priorities—athletes, coaches, and parents. Do this: Sit down with a pen and paper and ask yourself, "Why do I like sports? What makes me happy when I'm involved in sports?"

List everything (including winning and playing well). Consider things like being with people I like who share my passion; watching my children compete and have fun; enjoying the sporting venue (whether a beautiful golf course, youth soccer field, or classic stadium); the competitive nature of sports (win or lose); the exercise, recreation, and entertainment aspects; the excitement and spectacle of sporting events; learning about myself and others; developing skills; etc.

When you're done, give each item on your list a percentage with your total adding up to one hundred. It should help you to keep winning in perspective but, more importantly, help you to be happier the next time you play or watch a sporting event.

5

COLLEGE SPORTS:
WHERE DO WE GO FROM HERE?

Big-time college sport is filled with hypocrisy. Many NCAA administrators, college and university presidents, athletic directors, and coaches constantly talk about their educational values and the importance of "student-athletes" getting an education. But their actions speak louder than their words. Every decision they make seems to be driven by revenue-at-all-costs and win-at-all-costs motives, not educational ethos. That has to change.

Ralph Nader, founder, League of Fans

Today, athletics in our schools is increasingly about the end result—winning and money—rather than the process of education. As such, the potential of athletics as an educational tool has diminished greatly.

John Gerdy, longtime college sports administrator and sports
management professor

Let's face it. The world of big-time college sports is a mess. It's a world at the precipice of collapsing under the weight of ego- and greed-based policies and decision making. In a growing number of cases, any link between these college sports factories and the educational mission on our campuses is tenuous at best.

Anyone interested in intercollegiate athletics has become used to reading and hearing about the seemingly never-ending recruiting scandals, cases of academic fraud, and the cross-subsidization of athletics at the expense of academic programs. These scandals continue to happen year after year.

In recent years, three of the most storied football programs in the country—Miami, Ohio State, and USC—have been hit with major scandals.

And then there's the ugliness of the Penn State scandal, based around child molestation charges against a former assistant coach on the football staff. The Penn State case was the result of a complete institutional break-down—ethically and legally—and a widespread cover-up. It's another example of the power that athletic departments wield and the out-of-control culture of big-time college athletics.

The University of California-Berkeley has been embroiled in a controversy regarding the cross-subsidization of athletics for several years. A frustrated group of faculty members submitted a resolution, called Academics First, to the faculty senate asking the chancellor to stop subsidizing sports and to prioritize education. Not surprisingly, it passed handily.

Brian Barsky, a Cal-Berkeley professor and one of the two lead authors of Academics First, said he was motivated to action after discovering that intercollegiate athletics was receiving millions of dollars from the university administration and student fees. In fact, for the last two decades, the university administration has been contributing a few million dollars per year to Cal Athletics. Another roughly $2 million per year comes directly from student fees.

This is money that Cal-Berkeley could definitely use in various academic departments where budget cuts have been substantial. Instead the money is funneled to athletics in order to help feed the athletics arms race (stadium upgrade, new facilities, high-priced coaches, etc.) in big-time college sports. This type of cross-subsidization is not isolated to Cal-Berkeley. It's a common practice in NCAA Division I athletics.

Major college sports (primarily NCAA Division I football and men's basketball) have increasingly mimicked professional sports over the past twenty-five years. As such, there have been growing questions about whether commercialized college sports contribute to educational values in any meaningful way.

More and more, big-time college athletic departments are driven by WAAC and PAAC ethos, not educational ethos. How else to explain the fact that Division I athletic directors and football and men's basketball (and increasingly women's basketball) coaches are hired and fired almost exclusively based on revenue generated and win-loss records rather than anything remotely associated with education? Or the fact that the head football or men's basketball coach is almost always the highest paid employee on campus?

Major college sports have long transitioned from Education Sport, where educational concerns trump commercial concerns, to Entertainment Sport, where decisions are driven almost purely by commercial values.

As such, there are signs of growing unrest with the college sports complex among various constituencies. For example, in recent years, there have been calls from citizens, students, and college faculty members for Congress to examine whether or not big-time NCAA sports programs should be allowed to keep their tax-exempt status as educational entities, due to their highly commercialized and professionalized nature.

College athletes are beginning to organize and ask the NCAA, and the colleges and universities they attend, to treat them more fairly, including receiving more protection if injured while playing. There have been several instances of college athletes being forced to pay for some or all of the medical costs associated with an injury received while playing a sport for their school.

Additionally, hundreds of athletes have lost their athletic scholarships— despite doing well in the classroom—because their coaches have decided they're not scoring enough touchdowns or making enough baskets on the hardwood.

Economically, college football and basketball players continue to be exploited. According to a study by the National College Players Association (NCPA) and the Drexel University Sport Management Department, football and men's basketball players at top sports schools are being denied at least $6.2 billion between 2011 and 2015 under NCAA rules that prohibit them from being paid.

"America's economic system is supposed to operate on free markets," said UCLA quarterback Brett Hundley, an economics major. "This is a lesson on how damaging it can be when a cartel stifles a free market and, unfortunately, college athletes are the ones on the losing end. It's not right."

On another front, college faculty members are becoming increasingly concerned about what's happening on their campuses as incidents of academic corruption involving the athletic department damage the reputations of entire universities. The Drake Group, a consortium of faculty members across the country, was formed to combat the negative impact of big-time athletics on academics.

TELEVISION RULING SPURRED A NEW ERA

The commercialization and professionalization of college sports really took off in earnest in 1984 when the Supreme Court ruled that conferences and individual schools (read: Notre Dame) could negotiate their own TV deals. Division I conferences, primarily the big-time conferences that became known as the BCS (Bowl Championship Series) conferences (Big Ten, Pac-12, SEC, ACC, Big 12, Big East, along with Notre Dame), began cutting multimillion dollar deals with television networks for media rights to football and men's basketball games. As a result, the college sports arms race moved to full throttle.

Signs of the commercialization and professionalization of college sports are everywhere. CNNMoney.com estimated that at the completion of the 2010 season, college football had become a $2.2 billion annual business, a 28 percent increase since 2004. The University of Texas, as an individual entity, cut a $300 million deal with ESPN to form the Longhorn Network. In basketball, the NCAA signed a fourteen-year deal with CBS and Turner in 2010 for almost $11 billion, a 40 percent increase from the previous contract. The NCAA also has a $55 million annual agreement with ESPN to televise championship events of other sports, including the women's basketball tournament and the College World Series baseball championships.

Major college football coaches made an average of almost $1.5 million in 2011. That's an increase of approximately 55 percent since 2006. Mack Brown, the head football coach at the University of Texas, was making approximately $5 million a year at the time of his firing. Alabama's Nick Saban has a contract that pays him nearly $7 million a year. Meanwhile John Gagliardi, the head football coach at Division III Saint John's (Minnesota), the all-time winningest coach in college football history across all divisions, made only about 2.5 percent of Brown's salary when he retired after the 2012 season.

According to the book *Big Time Sports in American Universities*, by Duke professor Charles Clotfelter, the average salaries of football coaches at forty-four Division I schools rose from $273,300 in 1985–1986 to just over $2 million in 2009–2010.

According to a 2012 report in *USA Today*, athletic directors at FBS (Football Bowl Subdivision, formerly Division I-A) schools are paid an average of $515,000, an increase of 14 percent over 2011. Louisville's athletic director, Tom Jurich, was the highest paid athletic director at $1,401,915 annually.

Why are coaches and athletic directors paid so much? A big reason is because university athletic departments don't have to pay the workforce!

According to sports and culture writer Patrick Hruby, big-time college athletics is "a tax-evading, labor price-fixing cartel."

"When you don't have to pay competitive wages for your actual workforce, there's a lot more cash available to shower upon high-level bureaucrats," points out Hruby.

When you can hide under your nonprofit umbrella as an educational institution and avoid paying the taxes you should and when you don't have to pay your laborers a fair wage, you can splurge on things like lavish training facilities, giant video boards for stadiums and arenas, opulent suites, and more marketing people charged with bringing in more revenue. In fact, the money goes to everything within the athletic department except the athletes themselves.

This phenomenon is called "gold-plating" by economists, which basically means blowing money on unnecessary areas of the organization simply because the money is available to be spent.

In the case of college athletic departments operating under a nonprofit tax exemption as part of an educational institution, the money is spent because nonprofits technically can't turn a profit. Thus, the money has to go somewhere. Less money going to athletes means more money for salaries and extravagances throughout the athletic department.

"Division I college sports is big business," says sports journalist Dave Zirin. "Billions of dollars are generated, yet the people who give the blood and sweat to generate those dollars don't see a dime of it. It speaks to the deep problems and misplaced priorities we have in higher education in this country."

According to a study led by Ellen Staurowsky, a professor at Drexel University, the fair market value of a football player at the University of Texas for the 2011–2012 school year would be $567,922 annually. The calculation was based on an NFL-like shared revenue system. The value of a "full-ride" athletic scholarship at Texas was $21,090 a year at the time of her study. As such, the fair market value denied (the difference between the fair market value and the value of the scholarship) was $546,832.

The Texas football team generated $103.8 million in revenue. The cost of scholarships was $1.8 million. That leaves a lot of money left to blow on lavish facilities and to boost the salaries of coaches, administrators, and team chefs in the athletes' dorms.

While big-time athletic directors and coaches talk about their "student-athletes" and the importance of their educational values, the reality is athletic department policies and decisions are increasingly being made based on entertainment business objectives. We're left with a college sports system that—at the highest levels especially—is lacking in integrity and filled with hypocrisy.

College administrators today make no bones about running their athletic departments as business enterprises. For example, University of Colorado-Boulder chancellor Phil DiStefano made business acumen his top priority in searching for a new athletic director.

"I made the decision that now is the time to bring in a strong leader to set a strategy that will step the department up to a new level of performance and fundraising and overall management," said DiStefano. "I want an athletic director who will run the athletic department like a business. What's really key in athletics is big business, as we approach a budget of $50 to $60 million [annually] and see that growing each year. I want to make sure we have an AD who will run the athletic department like a business, *since we are a big business* [emphasis added]."

Others, including the University of Michigan, beat DiStefano to the punch, in terms of bringing a successful business leader on board to run the athletic department. Michigan hired David Brandon as its director of intercollegiate athletics in 2010. He was formerly chairman of the board and CEO of Domino's Pizza.

We've strayed so far from college athletics as an educational endeavor that we now hire pizza barons to run athletics.

LINKING BIG-TIME SPORTS WITH EDUCATIONAL INSTITUTIONS WAS THE ORIGINAL MISTAKE

Our college sports system has been ill-conceived from day one.

The United States is basically the only country in the world where elite athletic teams are sponsored by educational institutions (high schools and colleges), rather than by either government sports programs, large club sports organizations, or professional sports franchises, as is the case in other countries.

In most countries, colleges and universities offer physical education, intramural-type athletics programs, and maybe small club sports teams (usually student run), but nothing like what we see with big-time football and men's basketball in this country.

"Universities are ill-equipped to run a $6 billion entertainment business," says *New York Times* columnist Joe Nocera.

What we have at the NCAA Division I level, most notably in the large "Big Five" conferences, is a flawed system that makes it very hard for education to remain a priority in the athletic department and for college sports to be run in an ethical manner.

University of Chicago president Robert Maynard Hutchins saw the problem clearly way back in 1939 and decided to drop big-time football at his school because of the overt commercialism and lack of integrity involved in college sports at the time. A fifty-five-thousand-seat stadium on the Chicago campus was knocked to the ground.

"To be successful, one must cheat. Everyone is cheating and I refuse to cheat," said Hutchins.

Yet, other college presidents have failed to follow Hutchins' lead. In fact, a lot of them have exacerbated the problem. School presidents, with rare exceptions, have caved in to pressures from pro–Entertainment Sport interests. Often those pressures come from members of a school's board of trustees, who themselves have a warped view of campus priorities.

"It's about leadership," says John Gerdy, a longtime college sports administrator and professor turned reformer. "If there's any institution in society that needs to stand up and say education is more important than athletics, it has to be our universities. They have to provide leadership on athletics in education.

"Our education system is in crisis. In this global economy, the only way we're going to be successful as a country is to have a strong education system. Education has to be more important than athletics. But if you watch how some of our biggest universities act, you'd have to conclude that athletics are more important than education.

"The whole country is watching our colleges and universities. Part of the mission of our universities is to provide leadership on important issues impacting society. They're not doing that today when it comes to athletics in education."

THE FIRST STEP TO CHANGE IS RECOGNIZING THE REALITIES OF TODAY'S COLLEGE SPORTS LANDSCAPE

> Father Edward Malloy, former Notre Dame president, resigned when football coach Ty Willingham was fired at the behest of booster trustees because he wasn't winning enough games. He said publicly that he was "ashamed of his university," but the "Chair of the Board of Boosters" won the day. The real power at schools like Notre Dame doesn't lie in the president's office.
>
> William Dowling, Rutgers professor and winner of the
> Drake Group's Robert Maynard Hutchins Award for
> his work fighting corruption in college athletics

Taking the route Hutchins took at the University of Chicago is certainly a legitimate option for our major universities, perhaps the best option. Dropping big-time sports completely and only offering physical education, intramural sports, student-run club sports, and possibly Division III–type varsity sports (the University of Chicago eventually brought back varsity football at the Division III level some thirty years after Hutchins dropped it) would certainly be a rational move by college presidents and their boards of trustees.

Nonetheless, it's certainly acknowledged here that big-time varsity athletics are extremely popular with American sports fans and athletes. Millions of people love watching top-level college sports in person and on television. Thousands of youngsters dream of playing sports for their favorite colleges. Our university campuses are filled with mammoth football and basketball palaces. At this point, it would undoubtedly be very difficult to put the big-time college sports genie back in the bottle.

So, the challenge, at least for the time being, is to recognize the reality of big-time college sports' popularity and develop initiatives that will make college sports more honest, restore academic integrity on college campuses relative to athletics, and treat college athletes more fairly, ethically, and safely.

The NCAA's stated purpose is "to integrate intercollegiate athletics into higher education so that the educational experience of the student athlete is paramount."

Unfortunately, that mission statement is a joke at too many major universities when it comes to actual practice in big-time college athletics.

"The NCAA's amateur ideals are contrived," says civil rights historian and author Taylor Branch. "The NCAA is unstable and unbalanced in a number of respects. They represent about 1200 schools but all their attention is on the big BCS schools. The NCAA is divided between the big-time football and basketball programs and everyone else. There's a lot of financial infighting. The big schools resent the money from March Madness that's paid to the smaller schools.

"In terms of rules violations, the NCAA's enforcement with the big schools is getting weaker and weaker because the NCAA is afraid the big-time conferences and schools will leave and form their own organization. If you tell Ohio State you can't be on TV, you're talking about millions of dollars. Ohio State and the Big Ten wouldn't stand for it."

It's extremely doubtful that a highly commercialized and professionalized sports system, one that includes one hundred thousand–seat stadiums and multibillion dollar TV contracts, is the best way to pursue the NCAA's stated mission of making the "educational experience of the student athlete paramount."

"I thought all this conference realignment we've had in recent years was very sad," says former NFL player turned sports reformer Joe Ehrmann.

"Here we had presidents of universities, who are supposed to be protecting and promoting the mission of education, approving the pulling of their schools out of conferences solely to chase the TV money in two sports, football and men's basketball."

"Grow sports revenues at all costs." That continues to be the mantra of the leaders of our big-time sports universities.

The march toward greater and greater commercialization of big-time college athletics continues unabated. In an August 2014 power play, the sixty-five schools in the Power Five conferences (ACC, Big Ten, Big 12, Pac-12, and SEC) separated themselves from the rest of the NCAA's Division I programs in order to set their own rules. The result is basically a new informal power subdivision under the NCAA umbrella (these schools don't want to leave the NCAA altogether for fear of losing their tax-exempt status). The gap between the "haves" and "have-nots" in college athletics will now expand at a faster rate, as the Big Five conferences increasingly look more and more like the NFL and NBA than they do other NCAA conferences.

"Today, athletics in our schools is increasingly about the end result—winning and money—rather than the process of education," says Gerdy. "As such, the potential of athletics as an educational tool has diminished greatly. We need a serious conversation in this country about what the proper role is for sports in education.

"The most fundamental question is, 'What shall the role of sports be in our educational system?' We're heaping more and more money on football and basketball for entertainment purposes and pushing all the rest of the students to the sidelines—in the most obese society going! We need to get everyone in our schools participating in lifetime sports and other physical activities."

Dealing with the multitude of issues in college sports is frustrating. At times, it seems the state of college athletics is worse than ever. But with the increase in awareness of these issues, among not only sports fans, but the general public as a whole, comes hope.

"One thing's for sure, more people than ever are aware of the problems and issues in college sports today," says sports sociologist and sports management professor Allen Sack. "Looking back fifteen to twenty years, people thought I was crazy for raising a lot of these issues back then. Today, more people understand the issues. There has definitely been progress in terms of awareness. People realize there's a problem here between big-time college sports and higher education."

RECOMMENDATIONS

Reforming college sports is a huge challenge, perhaps the biggest challenge of any issue discussed in this book. The reason is the original ill-conceived model of tying high-level athletics to our educational institutions.

Marrying big-time sports to institutions of higher education can only result in trouble. And it certainly has. Moreover, any reform efforts of an ill-conceived college sports model will be by definition less than ideal.

Due to the complexity of the college sports problem—which has evolved primarily from the entertainment business ethos at its foundation—a tiered approach to reform is called for.

The following recommendations are made in an attempt to achieve three critical goals for college sports:

1. Enhanced academic integrity in college athletics
2. Economic and social justice for college athletes
3. Ethical and safe treatment of college athletes

The first eight recommendations are designed to simply improve the existing system. The NCPA, led by president Ramogi Huma, a former football player at UCLA, has done outstanding work in this area. Several of these recommendations have been adapted from NCPA proposals.

The ninth, and final, recommendation calls for a new economic model for college athletics to address the civil rights injustices inherent in the existing system. The "Last Alternatives" section outlines more drastic options if the first-tier recommendations are ignored by the NCAA and its member institutions.

I. Cover All Sports-Related Medical Expenses for Athletes and Disallow the Pulling of Scholarships from Athletes Who Suffer Injuries While Engaged in Sports Activities for Their School

Currently there are athletes losing their athletic scholarships (or having them reduced) due to injuries incurred during athletic competition for their university. That's simply wrong.

As the NCPA says, "It is immoral to allow a university to reduce or refuse to renew a college athlete's scholarship after sustaining an injury while playing for the university."

Even worse is the fact that some schools aren't paying for all—or part— of athletes' medical expenses that are clearly tied to college sports–related injuries. Both of those occurrences need to stop.

2. Require Athletic Scholarships to Cover the Full Cost of College Attendance

"Full" athletic scholarships should be just that and cover the full cost of college attendance for students.

According to an NCPA and Drexel University study, the average scholarship shortfall (out-of-pocket expenses) for each "full" scholarship athlete was approximately $3,222 per player during the 2010–2011 school year.

Many major college football and basketball players come from impoverished circumstances. The full cost of attendance should be covered under full athletic scholarship programs. The NCPA suggests that these additional scholarship costs could easily be covered by using a relatively small percentage of postseason revenues. That sounds reasonable.

3. Develop Policies That Severely Limit Weekday Games

Academic performance is hindered, and graduation rates are damaged, by the growing number of NCAA Division I games that take place on weekdays. In order to honor the NCAA's stated mission "to integrate intercollegiate athletics so that the educational experience of the student athlete is paramount," the number of weekday games needs to be curtailed significantly. Scheduling weekday football games is not in the best interests of students' educational work, nor are multiple midweek basketball games.

Moreover, the recent conference realignment frenzy that disregards the geographic location of schools results in not only football and basketball teams traveling greater distances to compete in games but women's soccer and men's lacrosse teams too. Conference realignment is clearly an anti-education trend in which PAAC thinking prevails.

4. Implement Standard Safety Guidelines across the NCAA to Prevent Avoidable Injuries, Illnesses, and Deaths

"Off-season" training and conditioning programs at college programs can be brutal at times. They can take away from academic efforts and also jeopardize the health of the athletes. For example, at the University of Iowa, thirteen football players were hospitalized after an extreme, over-the-top weightlifting exercise left some players so weak and dizzy they collapsed after the workout. The players were hospitalized with rhabdomyolysis, a muscle disorder that causes discolored urine and extreme soreness.

Shane DiBona, a freshman linebacker at Iowa, talked about the workout on Facebook: "I had to squat 240 pounds 100 times and it was timed. I can't walk and I fell down the stairs. . . life's great."

The Iowa sports information office released a statement on the matter:

> The Hawkeye football players admitted to the University of Iowa Hospitals and Clinics were all participating in NCAA allowable winter workouts. The symptoms, for which the student-athletes are being treated, are likely related to those workouts.

Iowa formed a special committee to investigate the situation. The type of weightlifting session used was eliminated permanently. Nobody involved was disciplined but the school took steps to educate employees, athletes, and others about how to prevent and identify rhabdomyolysis. The school said all thirteen players appear to have completely recovered and that it's possible, but unlikely, they will develop long-term health problems from the incident. If so, they'll be the lucky ones. Extreme off-season workouts have had worse outcomes in other cases, including death.

The NCPA states: "Several deaths in the college football off-season have highlighted the need for year-round safety requirements that provide an adequate level of protections for college athletes from all sports."

5. Extend California's "Student-Athlete's Right to Know Act" across the Nation

In October 2010 California governor Arnold Schwarzenegger signed "Student-Athlete's Right to Know Act" (AB 2079) into law. Most notably, this law now requires all California colleges and universities to publicly disclose their policies regarding sports-related medical expenses, standards for scholarship renewals, and out-of-pocket expenses that student-athletes on "full" athletic scholarship are expected to pay. In essence, it requires coaches to be transparent and honest with the seventeen-year-olds they're recruiting—and with their parents.

"The only way to know for sure what a university's policies are is to see something in writing," said NCPA president Huma, who helped drive the effort. "This is a historic milestone in college athletes' fight for basic protections. The NCPA will not stop until all athletic programs are forced to be honest with their recruits."

6. Establish Year-in-Residence Programs for Student-Athletes Admitted as "Special Admits"

For years freshmen were ineligible to compete in varsity NCAA athletics. That should be the case today for athletes (freshmen and transfers) admitted to universities and colleges on a "special admit" basis. Virtually all universities offer a small group of prospective students who don't qualify through the school's general admissions process "special admits" for various reasons. One of the big reasons for these special admits is to allow big-time college football and basketball programs opportunities to get athletes on their teams who wouldn't normally be accepted under a school's regular admission guidelines. A year-in-residence rule for special admits would allow these students to focus on their academic transition and send a strong message that the NCAA is serious about its mission statement.

This year-in-residence rule would allow special admits one school year to establish a solid academic base for their college career without the pressures of varsity competition. In addition, this rule would also improve graduation rates, a significant problem in big-time football and basketball programs.

Another likely outcome is that athletes qualifying only as "special admits," who aren't interested in a year-in-residence situation to establish their academic credentials, would be less likely to pursue the college sports route.

These athletes could look for other options (e.g., junior college, National Association of Intercollegiate Athletics [NAIA], pro sports leagues, overseas sports opportunities, etc.). This would free up NCAA openings for special admits who are truly interested in pursuing a college education.

In addition, reestablishing the year-in-residence policy for *all* freshmen should be seriously considered as well. It would help freshmen make the transition to college academically and socially. It would also help filter out athletes who aren't interested in getting an education. For example, basketball players might choose to go straight to pro basketball options overseas rather than sitting out their freshman year at college.

7. Protect Athletes from Overzealous Coaches and Athletic Directors by Either (1) Replacing the Existing One-Year Renewable Scholarship with a Five-Year Scholarship or (2) Eliminating the Athletic Scholarship Altogether and Moving to the Division III Model

The Drake Group believes colleges and universities "should be committed to athletes as students whose value to the university exceeds their role in athletics."

They've proposed replacing the one-year renewable (which also means "revocable") athletic scholarships currently in place with either multiyear scholarships or a need-based-only financial aid system (the Division III model).

Either option would be a positive development for several reasons. For one, it would empower student-athletes and protect them from overzealous coaches and athletic directors who currently have the power to drop athletes from scholarship due to injury or athletic performance—even if the athlete is excelling in the classroom. That's not a system that values athletes as students. It's a system that's unethical and unfair.

Multiyear scholarships were once allowed by the NCAA and should be again. The NCAA dropped multiyear scholarships in favor of one-year renewable scholarships in 1973. The move gave coaches and athletic directors more power and control over their athletes. The one-year renewable scholarship remains in place today despite huge increases in athletic department revenues.

Today, coaches have an excessive amount of control over athletes, on and off the playing fields and courts, including where they live, what they eat, when they eat, what campus activities they can partake in, and in some cases what classes they take. From the athletes' perspective, under a one-year revocable scholarship system, sports have to be their top priority on campus or they risk losing their financial aid.

Five-year scholarships would cover the student-athlete's four years of eligibility and a fifth year to cover the common practice of "redshirting" (sitting out a year to develop as a player, physically and mentally). For athletes who don't redshirt, a five-year scholarship would allow an extra year for completing a bachelor's degree if sports demands prevented the completion of degree requirements in the traditional four years. Moreover, some student-athletes might be able to finish a master's degree within five years, or at least complete significant work toward a graduate degree.

In addition, under this proposal, five-year scholarships could not be pulled due to injury or athletic performance reasons. A student who's fully meeting a school's academic standards, as well as team rules for his/her sport, should not have a scholarship pulled because the coach believes the student's athletic performance is subpar.

To increase the chances that this rule would be followed, all financial aid, including athletic scholarships, would be managed by the institution's financial aid office. Of course, coaches would retain the right to offer athletic scholarships to whomever they wish if the students meet NCAA and institution guidelines. However, after the athlete accepts the scholarship offer, management of the scholarship would move to the school's financial aid office.

The other option under this recommendation would be to drop athletic scholarships entirely and compete under NCAA Division III rules, which don't allow athletic scholarships.

It's a little-known fact today, but from 1906, when the organization was founded, until 1957, the NCAA didn't allow athletic scholarships of any kind. Student-athlete financial aid consisted of need-based aid or academic-merit scholarships only.

In effect, under a need-based-aid or academic-grants-only system, athletes in programs at this level would be treated like every other student on campus. Athletics would simply be an adjunct to the school's educational mission and athletes would be expected to be committed students first, athletes second.

Under this proposal, as with the five-year scholarship option, a student-athlete's financial aid (need based or academic based) would be controlled by the financial aid office, not the athletic department. As such, the student would retain his/her financial aid regardless of injury, athletic performance, or even if he/she decided to quit the sport at the varsity college level—as long as the student met the academic conditions of the financial aid award.

Moving away from the current one-year renewable scholarship to either a five-year scholarship system, or a system allowing need-based aid or academic-merit scholarships only, moves the needle back toward educational values in college athletics. It would also increase graduation rates among athletes as it would allow for more time for, and attention to, academics.

8. Implement the Wetzel College Football Play-off Plan in Lieu of the Old BCS or New Four-Team College Football Play-off Systems

> The BCS is a system based on blatantly exclusionary practices that curtails competition, reduces quality and is detrimental to college football fans (especially those rooting for [non-BCS] teams), to the [non-BCS] schools themselves, to the [non-BCS] team athletes (including those not on the football team due to the reduced revenue for the overall athletic program), as well as to the businesses and broadcasters who enter into contracts with college football programs. A play-off system would increase net consumer welfare.
>
> Andrew Zimbalist, professor of economics, Smith College

UNIVERSITY OF WINCHESTER
LIBRARY

The Bowl Championship Series (BCS) model for deciding the champion of college football's highest level was dismantled after the 2013 season. Good riddance. However, in its place is a flawed four-team play-off that needs to be the next target for dismantling.

The four-team play-off, adopted by college football's power brokers, maintains the "Big Five" conferences' unfair advantages over other Division I programs. In fact, the executive director of the old BCS, Bill Hancock, still runs the new four-team play-off.

A sixteen-team play-off is the most fair, fan-friendly, and player-friendly postseason option.

The "Wetzel Play-off Plan," as championed by sports journalist Dan Wetzel (coauthor of *Death to the BCS: The Definitive Case against the Bowl Championship Series*), should be implemented instead of the four-team play-off system.

THE WETZEL PLAY-OFF PLAN

- Sixteen-team play-off
- Champions from *all* eleven NCAA Division I football conferences earn an automatic bid to the play-offs.
- At-large invitations are given to five teams to complete the sixteen-team field. At-large teams would be selected by an NCAA basketball-like selection committee ("a group of highly engaged people using common criteria to pick and set the field").
- The games are played at the site of the higher seed until the title game.
- Ignore the bowl games—outside of nostalgia they offer no value to a play-off system. The bowls could continue outside the play-off system as a nonaffiliated business if they choose to do so.
- The championship game would be held at a neutral site like the NFL does with the Super Bowl. For historical and nostalgic reasons, the championship game could be held at the Rose Bowl every year.
- Play the first two rounds in December, break for final exams, hold the semifinals just after Christmas and the title game in early January. ("Wetzel's Play-off Plan: Money Talks" 12/7/09, Yahoo! Sports)

As Wetzel states, this plan, or one like it, would mean "never again would an unbeaten team be denied a chance to pursue a title." In addition to the more equitable competition factors, revenue distribution would be fairer—

and with a highly popular sixteen-team play-off, there would be more media revenue to share.

"Money we've got," says Wetzel. "Fairness we've got. Excitement we've got. A play-off plan that would solve all problems and create a four-week event that would rival the NFL play-offs in popularity, we even have that."

Let's make it happen.

9. A New Economic Model for College Sports

The eight recommendations here are a starting point. If they are implemented the current college sports system will be a much better place for athletes.

But the recommendations here don't completely address a huge issue, the economic injustice faced by the college athletes responsible for the multibillion-dollar industry known as college sports. Big-time college sports are a reality. While a University of Chicago–like de-emphasis of varsity athletics would likely be best for higher education in this country, the reality is it's not going to happen anytime soon.

Therefore, any serious college-sports-reform effort must address the prevailing economic injustice.

The hypocrisy in college athletes today is the result of an untenable system that promotes the amateur myth and tries to suppress the fact that the young athletes that fill the seats at football stadiums and basketball arenas on our college campuses have significant market value.

"The plight of college athletes is definitely a civil rights issue," says Branch. "The governance of college sports is a civil rights issue because the athletes are citizens and are being denied their rights by what amounts to collusion. Colleges are telling football and basketball players they can't get anything above a college scholarship. The athletes are being conned out of their rights. We need modern abolitionists to fight this unjust and unstable system."

For decades, college-sports-reform initiatives have ignored the strong marketplace demand for star football and basketball players coming out of high school. With such strong demand for these highly skilled athletes, an underground economy inevitably will develop to compensate the athletes. Amateurism, a form of prohibition, simply won't work in a marketplace with such high demand.

What's needed is an overhaul in NCAA policies, rules, and regulations when it comes to the benefits college athletes can receive. Athletes deserve to share in the wealth created due to their efforts on the courts and fields of our universities.

The question is how should they share in the wealth? What's the best system? Some have suggested that athletes be paid salaries like athletes in the NFL, NBA, MLB, and NHL. However, that brings up a host of issues; for example, how will athletes in nonrevenue sports like swimming and tennis be dealt with? What are the Title IX ramifications? Will an athletes' union need to be formed to negotiate compensation? If so, how will it operate and whom will the union negotiate with? What about worker's compensation issues? Clearly, a system in which college athletic departments paid athletes a salary would require dealing with a complex web of factors.

There's a better and easier way: Let athletes have the right to benefit from use of their names, images, and likenesses—like every other student at our colleges and universities. College athletic departments don't need to put athletes on the payroll. But athletes should be allowed to take endorsement money like the coaches who lead them. If the local auto parts store wants to pay a college athlete to sign autographs for two hours during a store sale, why shouldn't the athlete be allowed to take that opportunity? If someone wants to give an athlete a gift—be it cash or tattoos—why should that be banned? Music students in college are free to accept cash or gifts for playing a weekend gig at the local club. What makes athletes different?

"Is it so ignoble for a college athlete to make money off his or her talent and fame?" asks sports and culture writer Patrick Hruby. "Nobody in America has to deal with the restrictions on income that the NCAA imposes. Actors and musicians can go off to college, be on scholarship, and still make money off their talent. It's morally wrong, and un-American, to prevent athletes from doing the same."

It's time to eliminate this outdated concept of amateurism and allow college athletes to be compensated for having their pictures on calendars, for example. It's time to allow the so-called "money handshakes." What other college students are banned from taking gifts? There aren't any.

Prohibition, in the form of the amateurism myth, doesn't work. The underground economy in college sports will only grow as the money in college sports grows.

Dumping the amateur myth isn't a new concept. As Hruby and *New York Times* columnist Joe Nocera have eloquently and consistently pointed out, the Olympics dumped the amateur myth and allowed athletes to make money from their athletic ability and fame. And guess what? The world didn't end! In fact, the Olympics are more popular than ever.

"The current system basically screws a bunch of kids, a lot of them dis-advantaged kids," says Nocera.

Paying athletes salaries as university employees is impractical, given the complex set of ancillary issues that option raises. However, allowing college athletes to receive money from outside the athletic department is much more straightforward.

In fact it's fair and just. And it gets rid of a lot of the hypocrisy in college sports.

"The moral unsustainability of college athletics, as it is presently struc-tured, is a huge issue," says Hruby. "There's a huge college sports economy that for the most part the athletes are left out of. . . . The myth of amateur-ism has to go. If the NCAA isn't going to pay the athletes directly—which admittedly is very tricky, a lot of things would have to be worked out—then at least administrators have to stop telling college athletes that they can't earn money from outside sources."

Exactly.

ANTITRUST LAWSUITS MIGHT CHANGE THE SYSTEM

What's the spur that will dramatically change the system?

Frederick Douglass once said, "Power concedes nothing without a de-mand."

It's a great quote. However, most of the time, demands—even of the loud variety—won't do the trick.

People in power, especially those with economic power, don't change the models that have given them an advantageous position without being forced to. Historically, one of the best ways to force change in America has been through lawsuits.

A big step forward came in August 2014 when federal judge Claudia Wilken issued a ruling in the landmark *O'Bannon v. NCAA* antitrust lawsuit filed in 2009 by a former UCLA All-American basketball player named Ed O'Bannon and a few other former college athletes. Basically, Wilken ruled that the NCAA was illegally prohibiting college athletes from profiting from the use of their names, images and likenesses in video games and television broadcasts.

It was a scary ruling for NCAA power brokers because in essence it critically wounded the NCAA's archaic and unfair amateurism model. However, the NCAA will undoubtedly try to keep the O'Bannon case and similar antitrust lawsuits tied up in the courts for years to come through the appeals process and other legal tactics.

Nevertheless, due to legal, political, media, and general public pressures, the NCAA will eventually have to meet with its opponents and do something they've resisted for decades: change the system.

"The NCAA will hopefully never be the same," said lead O'Bannon lawyer Michael Hausfeld after Wilken's ruling. "It's going to go through a metamorphosis and if it approaches it wisely, it should sit down and discuss with all the interested entities how best to form a new way going forward."

THE LAST ALTERNATIVES

> I don't think college athletics can survive the way things are going now. I think at some point a judge somewhere will rule that these kids are really professional athletes and employees and should be eligible for worker's compensation, etc. Or Congress will look at Division I athletics and determine that it's clearly a highly commercial enterprise and pull the tax-exempt status from these athletic programs. Either event would be financially devastating for university athletic programs and would cause universities to pull back and put college athletics in their proper perspective.
>
> John Gerdy, longtime college sports
> administrator and sports management professor

If the proposed reform recommendations outlined here—or measures very similar in nature—aren't implemented, radical change will be required. The current system simply isn't sustainable.

If NCAA executives and university administrators fail to move on these issues in the next couple of years, it will be time to take collective action as a society and give our universities an ultimatum. The ultimatum would basically entail selecting one of the following three alternatives regarding university athletics programs:

1. Drop intercollegiate varsity athletics altogether, offering students only physical education classes, intramural sports, and student-run club sports programs. The European model, if you will.
2. Place all intercollegiate athletics under the Division III model (no athletic scholarships; sports for educational, not entertainment, objectives; and the use of fields and courts as classrooms designed to sup-

plement the educational mission and foster the personal development of the participants). In effect, athletes in programs moving to the Division III level would be treated like every other student on campus. Financial aid would be based on need or academic merit. Athletics would simply be an adjunct to the school's educational mission and athletes would be expected to be students first, athletes second.

3. Reclassify athletic departments as for-profit entities. To that end, big-time college athletic departments' nonprofit, tax-exempt status would be removed. Once the nonprofit tax-exempt status of these entertainment business entities is removed, big-time university athletic departments would be reclassified as *for-profit* sports subsidiaries underneath the university umbrella.

Colleges and universities currently receive special tax treatment because they are educational institutions. As such, they are considered nonprofits and receive tax-exempt status, meaning their income is exempt from taxation. Also, gifts to these schools are usually tax-deductible. In addition, new arenas and stadiums are often built with tax-exempt bonds.

This special tax treatment for colleges and universities seems reasonable in cases where these institutions are clearly conducting academic activities as part of their educational mission. However, big-time college football and basketball programs are multibillion dollar enterprises. Education plays a secondary role to revenue and public relations objectives in these programs. In addition to the revenue generated by media rights, these schools make large sums of money from ticket sales, sales of club seats, luxury suites, personal seat licenses, advertising/sponsorship, championship tournaments, bowl games, and other revenue streams.

Clearly, these big-time sports programs are subsidiary businesses for the colleges and universities that operate them. Why should they receive tax-favored status?

If significant reform measures—such as those outlined earlier—aren't taken, the answer will clearly be: "They shouldn't."

6

PHYSICAL EDUCATION AND SPORTS FOR ALL STUDENTS

It's mind-boggling that at a time when overweight and obesity levels are up among our young people and physical activity levels are down, our schools are cutting physical education classes and intramural sports programs. Pressures driven by the No Child Left Behind legislation have led to cutbacks in physical education despite research that shows students receiving daily physical education are not only healthier but perform better academically. We need a concerted effort to increase quality fitness-based daily physical education classes, along with a return to the vibrant intramural sports programs our schools once offered.

Ralph Nader, founder, League of Fans

A NATION OF SPORTS SPECTATORS

As a country, we've never been fatter. More than 65 percent of adults in the United States are either overweight or obese.

That's sad. But what's even sadder is our children are on pace to be significantly fatter than we are by the time they reach adulthood. The Centers for Disease Control and Prevention reports that the percentage of children ages six to eleven who are overweight has increased nearly 300 percent during the past twenty-five years. The numbers are worse for teenagers.

Over the last three decades, the number of overweight adolescents has quadrupled. As a result, children today have a shorter life expectancy than their parents for the first time in one hundred years, according to William J. Klish, professor of pediatrics at the Baylor College of Medicine.

"We are in the middle of an epidemic that may have profound health effects for our children," Klish said. "If society doesn't act now to implement preventative measures, the increase of obesity will not stop."

The overall health implications are certainly scary. For example, type 2 diabetes once was considered an adult disease, hence the label "adult-onset diabetes." However, because more kids are overweight and obese, the incidence of the disease has increased dramatically in children and adolescents.

If current trends hold, diabetes is expected to afflict a third of the population by 2050 (obesity, a prime cause of diabetes, will afflict half the population by 2030). The expected *annual* cost of diabetes in 2034, according to a recent academic study, is $336 billion.

Adults and children need to move more and watch less. We're a sports-crazed nation but only when it comes to spectator sports. Collectively, in terms of participation in sports and other physical activities, we're a bunch of couch potatoes. Our cultural focus on top-level athletes—Entertainment Sport—deserves a substantial part of the blame.

We're a country of passionate sports fans who, for the most part, aren't sports participants. Sports fans tend to exercise less than the rest of the population and have riskier dietary habits. A study published in the United States Sports Academy's *The Sports Journal* supports this lifestyle profile of the American sports fan.

"Highly identified sports fans had significantly higher health risk behaviors than non-sports fans on a range of health behavior measures, including: higher fat consumption, more fast food consumption, less vegetable consumption, greater consumption of refined as opposed to whole grains, and an increased amount of alcohol consumed on days they chose to drink," according to the study's authors, Daniel R. Sweeney and Donna G. Quimby. "Additionally, using height and weight data to calculate Body Mass Index (BMI), highly identified sports fans were found to have a higher BMI."

Sweeney and Quimby suggest that since sports fans were found to engage in riskier health-related behaviors, they could be a prime target for health policy makers looking to positively impact a large segment of Americans while reducing health-care costs associated with obesity and other chronic health conditions. They also note an opportunity for pro sports organizations, college athletic departments, and individual professional athletes to embark on cause-related marketing campaigns encouraging healthier life-styles on the part of their fans.

"Partnering in programs designed to educate their most devoted follow-ers about strategies towards achieving a healthy lifestyle would serve the dual role of contributing to the overall success of the organization while at the same time positively impacting the health of those in the communities they serve," concluded Sweeney and Quimby.

Meanwhile, the nation's middle schools and high schools are focusing on varsity athletic teams that impact a relatively small percentage of the student population, while simultaneously cutting physical education classes and intramural sports programs that reach all students.

This situation needs to be turned on its head. In an era of increasing childhood obesity, our schools need to reverse their priorities in this area and focus on creating more physical education, sports, and other physical activity opportunities for the student body at large. Varsity sports programs should be a secondary consideration in schools that exist for educational purposes. Schools shouldn't be in the business of developing elite-level athletes while the majority of students within their walls are becoming increasingly inactive. Moreover, schools have no business in the sports entertainment business. Too many schools act like they're responsible for providing sports entertainment for the local community.

"Instead of increasing participation opportunities for all, we're subsidiz-ing football in our schools," says John Gerdy, a longtime athletic adminis-trator and sports management professor. "That just doesn't make sense, especially when you consider that the vast majority of football players will never participate in another game of football after high school."

PHYSICAL INACTIVITY IS THE PRIMARY CULPRIT

The rise in obesity rates in this country in general, and childhood obesity in particular, is caused by a complex set of factors. In addition to a significant drop in physical activity the last twenty-five years and an increase in empty calories, the tremendous growth in the use of high fructose corn syrup ("the fast-fat sugar") and partially hydrogenated oils is partly responsible.

The financial incentive of food companies is to find cheaper ingredients with longer shelf life—not to make their products healthier. Fast-food chains and convenience stores thrive on serving food with limited nutri-tional value. These foods, containing high fructose corn syrup, partially hydrogenated oils, MSG, and other unhealthy additives, are pumped up by the food industry's marketing machine via advertisements that often target our young people.

While acknowledging the role poor nutrition plays in the obesity epidemic, the decline in physical activity and fitness levels among our young people is a key factor in our nation's deteriorating state of wellness, and it may very well be the most important one.

"Research has shown that lack of physical activity may be a more significant factor in contributing to childhood obesity than even bad diet," according to former congressman and NBA player Tom McMillen. "Other research in adults," he adds, "indicates that poor fitness is a more significant predictor of death than obesity generally, diabetes and other causes. In other words, the most important thing we can do for the health of our kids is to get them up off the couch."

McMillen is chairman of the National Foundation for Physical Fitness, Sports and Nutrition. The foundation's mission is to generate private sector support to supplement the programs and budget of the President's Council on Physical Fitness, Sports and Nutrition. It is hoped that the foundation's efforts will spearhead a national commitment to increasing sports participation and bring much-needed resources to fighting our physical inactivity and obesity epidemic.

THE NUMBER OF PHYSICAL EDUCATION CLASSES IS DROPPING

A particularly disturbing part of the childhood obesity epidemic is the fact that the number of physical education (PE) classes in our schools is steadily declining, despite an array of experts stressing that more activity is crucial if kids are to achieve a healthy weight.

"The decline in physical education, recess, and intramural sports in schools is awful," says famed sportswriter Frank Deford. "The citizenry should be concerned about that."

The trend continues to go in the wrong direction. New elementary schools in parts of Georgia are being built without gyms today.

Thirty-five years ago, daily physical education was the norm for K–12 students. Today, according to the American Heart Association, only 4 percent of elementary schools, 7 percent of middle schools, and 2 percent of high schools have daily physical education class for the entire school year. Moreover, 22 percent of schools don't require physical education class at all!

The amount of time students spend in physical education steadily declines from kindergarten through high school. By high school, most kids in our country are basically done with PE. The result is that elementary school kids—who are increasingly overweight and obese themselves—are now 24 percent more active than high school students.

Due to No Child Left Behind mandates and standardized state assessment tests, many schools are cutting back on physical education and recess under the mistaken belief that kids need more desk time to improve test scores. Based on the latest research on exercise and the brain, that's the direct opposite approach that schools should be taking.

"Overall, I don't think there's any doubt that schools are feeling pressure from No Child Left Behind and standardized tests," according to Brenda VanLengen, vice chair of PE4life, a physical education advocacy organization. "In response, they are doing things like dropping PE classes in order to create more time in the classroom. Instead, they should be getting kids more *ready to learn* through more quality physical education and physical activity during the school day. Based on the research, their current approach is misguided.

"If each school would incorporate quality fitness-based PE programs—ideally daily, but at least three days a week—we would have healthier kids, academic performance would go up, and behavioral problems would drop. The research has consistently proven this."

THE FOCUS OF YOUTH SPORTS IS INCREASINGLY ON THE BEST ATHLETES

Physical education is only one side of the physical fitness coin for kids. The other side is youth sports programs. For very young kids, youth sports opportunities abound. But as children get older, the emphasis changes from "participation for all" to "participation for elite-level athletes." As a result, too many young people are pushed to the sidelines where they become sedentary spectators.

At issue is an elite sports mentality across our country's school system that values opportunities for the best athletes at the expense of participation for all. Interscholastic athletic teams continue to be sacred cows at most schools. Meanwhile, intramural sports programs, designed for the participation of all students, continue to disappear.

As a whole, the United States is one of the worst countries on the planet in terms of lifelong sports participation. A small percentage of us play the games and the rest of us watch. The problem starts early. While the number of boys and girls (ages five to twelve) participating in youth sports programs is strong, nearly 80 percent of them have dropped out of organized sports programs by thirteen.

This is unfortunate because the teen years are a time when sports participation can have its greatest benefits. Multiple studies show that teens who participate in sports are less likely to smoke, consume illegal drugs and alcohol, miss classes, have behavioral issues, drop out of school, suffer from anxiety and depression, and get pregnant. In addition, for those involved in sports, self-esteem tends to rise, grades improve, and the ability to solve problems, handle adversity, and be creative improves.

"I think the biggest problem is that kids don't make the high school team, or the junior high school team, and drop out," says Richard Lapchick, founder of the Center for the Study of Sport in Society at Northeastern University and currently director of the Institute for Diversity and Ethics in Sports at the University of Central Florida. "Kids think that if they don't make the team, that their career is over, therefore they should stop competing or playing or doing anything that makes them physically fit."

Drew Hyland, author of *Philosophy of Sport*, sees part of the solution being the development of a European-like sports club system. "I think what would be a wonderful thing would be for the United States to develop a more active sports club system of the sort that you see in Europe where folks keep on playing actively in leagues and so forth on into adulthood," says Hyland.

In most European countries, there is a sports club for everyone. If you're a premier athlete, there's a club team for you. If you're an athletically challenged child, but still love the game, there's also a team for you. Sports clubs in Europe often will have an "A" team, a "B" team, a "C" team, on down, so everyone's accommodated, including adults looking for competitive and recreational sports opportunities. Conversely, in the United States, club teams are primarily reserved for young top-level athletes. It would be wise for the United States—as part of an initiative to get more Americans participating in sports and not just watching them—to adopt the European model and develop a club sports system that more easily allows for sports participation from childhood through adulthood.

"Play is an elemental part of who we are as human beings," says sports journalist Dave Zirin. "The key is that we have to increase access to sports as much as possible so more of us can play, and continue playing. As a society, we've separated those who play and those who don't play. Any sports movement worth its salt has to break down that division between those who play and those who don't."

That said, while efforts certainly should be made to get our adults more active in sports, adult behavior is tough to change. As a country, our focus needs to be on getting our young people moving more through quality physical education, intramurals, and club sports, as well as other physical activities.

It's important to note that young people who are active through high school are more active than their less active school peers through their adult years. Active children tend to turn into active adults.

SHOULD VARSITY SPORTS PROGRAMS BE PART OF OUR SCHOOLS?

> If a cost/benefit analysis was done on the advantages of investing more in health and fitness classes in our schools and less on interscholastic sports, what would we see in terms of reduced costs to our society in the present epidemics of heart disease, obesity, colon cancer, diabetes and high blood pressure?
>
> Bruce Svare, author of *Reforming Sports before the Clock Runs Out*

In the United States, resources start getting directed toward programs for top-level athletes—both in schools and youth club organizations—at an early age.

In American high schools, only a minority of the total student population participates in varsity athletics. Yet, for the most part, schools' varsity sports teams have survived, and even prospered, during the nationwide school system budget crunch of the past decade.

In a time of a health-threatening childhood obesity epidemic, do we, as a society, want to prioritize varsity sports programs that only serve a school's best athletes over physical education and intramural sports programs that can benefit the entire student body?

When our educational system slashes physical education and intramural programs, the least athletic and less athletically inclined students are often left with few sports and physical activity options. It's simply poor public policy during a childhood obesity epidemic to fund a varsity athletic program for the benefit of a relatively small portion of the student body while cutting back on physical education and intramural sports programs positively impacting the majority of a school's students.

"Cutting PE to fund varsity athletics programs for the athletically inclined would be akin to only providing core academic courses (mathematics, science, etc.) to the intellectually gifted," says VanLengen.

A few courageous college administrators are moving in the opposite direction: de-emphasizing varsity athletics in order to fund sports and physical education programs for all students, not just the elite athletes on campus. Spelman College, in Atlanta, Georgia, took it a step further when they completely dropped varsity athletics in order to establish a campus-wide wellness program emphasizing physical education, intramural sports, and lifelong physical activity for *all* students.

It's important to note that physical fitness isn't just about healthier bodies. A growing mound of research is consistently revealing that as students' fitness levels rise, so do their academic test scores. The more fit students are, the better they perform academically. They also have fewer behavioral and emotional issues and miss school less often. Shouldn't those be important objectives for all college and high school administrators? A quality, cardiovascular-based physical education program, along with a full-fledged intramural sports and physical activity program, can go a long way toward those objectives.

Given our cultural tradition of linking top-level athletics with educational institutions, varsity athletics could still have a place on middle school, high school, and college campuses, but only if a "sports and PE for all" initiative is the top priority and fully funded.

One policy that would help justify varsity athletic programs while increasing overall student participation rates in sports is to implement a "no-cut" policy for all varsity sports programs offered by a given school.

Schools should be about providing learning opportunities for students. Cutting a group of students from school sports teams—in effect telling them that they aren't good enough to learn or improve at a sport—isn't an appropriate educational practice.

In public school classrooms, teachers can't discriminate on the basis of ability. They're required to accept and instruct all students. Why do we allow coaches to discriminate on the basis of ability—especially in public schools funded by tax dollars?

In schools that don't have intramural sports programs and/or little or no physical education requirements, "no-cut" policies are even more necessary.

As a society, we need to fully understand and appreciate that when it comes to the importance of physical activity for health and well-being, we're all athletes.

"Most nations fund sports in a true pyramid fashion, with lots of money at the base for youth grassroots participation and little at the top for elite athletics," says McMillen. "In America, we have inverted the pyramid. We

provide little at the base for community sports and school physical education programs for our children, while lavishing public subsidies at the top,
for example giving vast amounts of tax dollars to build professional sports
stadiums. If we want to win the fight against child obesity, we must flip this
pyramid and devote real resources to youth grassroots efforts."

THE NAPERVILLE MODEL

According to a report from the secretary of health and human services
and the secretary of education entitled *Promoting Better Health for Young
People through Physical Activity and Sports*, "Enhancing efforts to promote physical activity and sports among young people is a crucial national
priority."

We must have more physical education classes in our schools, not less,
as is the current trend. And we need more recreation and intramural programs that provide organized sports opportunities for all students, regardless of athletic ability.

"Serious consideration must be given to a school sports model that would
allow the resources, effort, time, and emotion currently showered upon
elite programs to be reallocated in ways that would more directly benefit
a much larger number of students," says Gerdy. "This would require an
increased emphasis on broad-based participation in activities that can be
practiced for a lifetime for purposes of promoting public health through
the expansion of physical education requirements, intramural and wellness
programs."

Naperville, Illinois School District #203, is an example of a school system
that gets it. It funds a high-quality, fitness-based, daily physical education
program that provides all students an opportunity to explore a variety of
team sports, individual sports, and other physical activities. The physical
education program stresses the mind-body connection and how regular
exercise enhances wellness, academic performance, and behavior. A vibrant
intramural sports program also exists as an option for Naperville students. A
high-quality varsity athletics program is also part of the Naperville equation.

Naperville's wellness and academic results are both outstanding. Consider that while nationally 30 percent of U.S. schoolchildren are overweight,
typically only 5 to 10 percent of Naperville school kids are overweight in any
given year. Naperville's focus on exercise and physical activity has paid off
in the classroom as well. Naperville students took the well-known TIMSS
(Trends in International Mathematics and Science Study) test and scored

number one in the world in science and number six in math on a worldwide basis. As a whole, U.S. students rank eighteenth in science and nineteenth in math on this assessment.

In one Naperville study, students who took a literacy class immediately following a physical education class improved an average of 1.4 years in grade-level equivalency versus 0.9 for students who took the literacy course only. Counselors at Naperville Central High School are so convinced of exercise's positive impact on the brain that they encourage all students to take their toughest class immediately following physical education.

The Naperville #203 school district has also had outstanding success with its varsity athletic program, winning numerous league, regional, and state honors. It doesn't necessarily have to be either/or when it comes to varsity sports and PE. Varsity programs are fine, *if* physical education and intramural sports options for *all* students are the priority.

Naperville proves that you can have an outstanding daily physical education program, a varied intramural program, and an excellent varsity athletic program. However, the physical education program is priority one and is a centerpiece of their educational curriculum. Because of the school PE program's positive impact on learning—in addition to the health and wellness benefits—Naperville calls its physical education program "learning readiness" PE.

The Naperville model, initiated by the "father of the new PE," Phil Lawler, has proven so popular that contingents from eleven foreign countries and forty-two states have visited Naperville to learn about the program and how they can replicate it in their home communities. Moreover, a PE4life physical education program, based on the Naperville model, has met with great success in a variety of socioeconomic situations: in small farming communities (e.g., Grundy Center, Iowa), old industrial towns (e.g., Titusville, Pennsylvania) and economically disadvantaged urban areas (e.g., Kansas City, Missouri). These schools have found fitness levels up, disciplinary incidents down, and academic performance on the rise.

RECOMMENDATIONS

I. Implement Legislation Requiring Quality Fitness-Based Daily Physical Education Programs That Are Designed for All Students, Not Just the Athletically Inclined, in Our Nation's Schools (K–12)

It used to be the one place that *all* kids could participate in sports and fitness activities was in physical education class. However, with cutbacks in PE classes over the past twenty-five years, that isn't the case today.

Physical education on a once-per-week basis is now the norm, and in some schools, kids go an entire semester—or even an entire school year—without a single day of physical education. Recess time is also being cut in elementary schools across the country. Pressures from the No Child Left Behind legislation—along with the annual state academic assessments the legislation has spawned—have led to the decline in physical education, art, music, and other "specials."

Our schools are driving in reverse here. Given all the research data showing that fit kids perform better academically and that exercise primes the brain for learning, our schools should be *adding* physical education classes, recess time, intramurals, before-school physical activity programs, and in-class exercises ("brain breaks"), not slashing these things.

"Exercise is like Miracle-Gro for the brain," says Dr. John Ratey, author of *SPARK: The Revolutionary New Science of Exercise and the Brain*. "It grows brain cells."

It's not as if our young people are getting plenty of physical activity outside of school. Over 75 percent of U.S. children are not active even twenty minutes a day. That's shocking. And tragic.

Physical education continues to be cut back and treated as the ugly stepchild in schools across the country, despite a worsening childhood obesity epidemic; despite a growing mound of evidence pointing to physical inactivity as the primary cause of the epidemic; despite the numerous benefits of quality daily physical education; despite over a decade of "calls to action" from the surgeon general, top health and education organizations, and numerous political leaders and despite a strong majority of teachers and parents who believe PE should be a big part of the childhood obesity solution. The bottom line is America's children need more physical activity. We're at a point in our nation's history when the need to teach our kids the benefits of a lifelong, physically active lifestyle has never been greater.

A major step forward would be to implement quality daily physical education programs in all of our schools, kindergarten through twelfth grade.

Phil Lawler, a leader in the fitness-based PE movement, described quality physical education this way:

It's about enabling each student to maintain a physically active lifestyle forever. It means emphasizing fitness and well-being, not athleticism. It eliminates practices that humiliate students. And it assesses students on their progress in reaching personal physical activity and fitness goals. A quality PE program exposes kids to the fun and long-term benefits of movement—it's really that simple.

According to an American Heart Association (AHA) position statement:

> Schools can play a critical role in increasing physical activity by offering qual-
> ity, daily physical education and other opportunities to recreate. Physical edu-
> cation not only gives children an opportunity to be active but it teaches them
> the skills they need to be active throughout their lifetime. Thus, investing in
> quality physical education in all schools for all grades is a logical and important
> step toward improving the health of the next generation.

The AHA recommends a *minimum* standard of 150 minutes a week of
physical education for elementary students and 225 minutes a week for
middle school students. It also recommends that the successful completion
of physical education be a requirement for high school graduation.

Dr. Kenneth Cooper, the "father of aerobics" and founder of the Cooper
Aerobics Center in Dallas, Texas, says the benefits of quality daily PE go
beyond improved health and wellness.

"Students at schools with daily fitness-oriented physical education programs are reaping the benefits of being physically fit: (1) improved health;
(2) higher academic performance; and (3) fewer behavioral problems,"
says Cooper. "There's more good news. Exercise has also been shown to
improve attention span and focus, lower anxiety and depression levels, and
raise self-esteem."

The characteristics of a quality PE program are:

- Provides daily physical education
- Meets the needs of all students, not just the athletically inclined
- Motivates children to embrace health and fitness for a lifetime
- Provides a wide variety of health and fitness activities, including indi-
  vidual and team sports, to promote an active lifestyle
- Provides authentic, individualized assessment—including fitness test-
  ing and cognitive testing—as a meaningful part of the learning process,
  empowering students to value and oversee their personal lifetime fitness
- Incorporates technology (e.g., heart-rate monitors, pedometers, "ex-
  erlearning" games, etc.) into physical education on a regular and continuing basis
- Grades on effort and fitness knowledge, not athletic ability (source:
  PE4life)

These components of a quality PE program, combined with the AHA
recommendations above, should provide the foundation for legislation

requiring quality daily physical education in every state, for every school, K–12. It needs to be a funded mandate.

It simply requires a reorienting of our national priorities. For NFL, MLB, NBA, and NHL teams, we've contributed billions of dollars in public funds to build the current stadiums and arenas around the league. A relatively small percentage of this financial outlay would fund high quality, fitness-based, academic-performance-enhancing physical education in K–12 schools across the country.

As another example, the federal antidrug war has cost Americans $44 billion a year, according to Harvard research. Yet illicit drug use has not declined after decades of a war on drugs costing billions of dollars. Surely, a big chunk of that money could be redirected toward quality daily physical education for our nation's schoolchildren. These physical education programs could include health education components that address the dangers of illicit drug use. Moreover, research has shown that fit kids have fewer behavioral problems, including drug use.

Once again, it's about priorities. Quality daily cardiovascular-based physical education will make our young people healthier (saving us billions in future costs associated with diabetes and other obesity-related problems), smarter (fit kids perform better on academic assessments), and better behaved (fit kids have fewer behavioral problems and fewer instances of depression and anxiety).

2. Schools at All Levels (K–12) Need to Develop and Implement Comprehensive Intramural Programs That Include a Variety of Team Sports, Individual Sports, and Other Lifetime Physical Activity Options

The fact is fewer young people are involved in sports today because our schools have steadily dropped their intramural programs over the past twenty-five years while protecting varsity sports programs from significant budget cuts. Private-club sports programs have evolved to provide elite athletes with even more options but kids who are less athletic, or can't invest the time or money in club sports programs, have fewer options today because physical education and intramural programs in schools have been slashed.

"Quite simply, American schools are not delivering enough physical activity programs, including intramural sports, that engage students and entice them away from competing attractions," says Scott A. G. M. Crawford, professor in the College of Education and Professional Studies at Eastern Illinois University.

Students say the interest is there but opportunities are lacking.

"Some kids want to participate in athletics for fun, but at most schools, especially at the high school level, participation in athletics is about winning," said Stephen Moon, an Eastern Connecticut State University student.

We have a "sports gap" in our schools and it's widening. The gap is between elite athletes, who have more opportunities than ever, and less athletically inclined students, who have fewer opportunities than ever before. At a time when we have a growing childhood obesity epidemic, that fact represents a serious error in judgment by policy makers in the education and sports realms.

"As a society, Americans appear to be at the two extremes of athletic participation," says Craig Stewart, professor and chair of the Department of Health and Human Development at Montana State University. "Either our children are playing on numerous competitive sport teams (often at the same time), or they are physically doing as little as possible away from the television or computer. There should be some effort to improve the cultural value on participation for the 'fun' of it."

Intramural sports programs were once a significant component of the educational offerings at most schools in this country. Those programs gradually went away as schools increasingly focused on developing elite athletes. As the pressure to boost varsity athletics budgets increased and school budgets in general tightened, intramurals were seen as an easy budget cut.

As a result, a lot of young people interested in sports for fun and fitness have been left behind.

"These programs [middle school and high school intramurals] provide a positive, uplifting environment where students participate for more intrinsic reasons," says Cassy Freeman, a student at Boise State University. "It gives these students an opportunity to stay physically active without the feelings of pressure and fear they may encounter in interscholastic sport programs."

The National Intramural Sports Council (NISC) describes the value of intramural programs this way:

Intramural/recreational sports programs as a part of the school curriculum ensure that all children are provided the opportunity, regardless of athletic skill level, to learn an energetic approach to life that can contribute to their enjoyment of leisure and maintain a style of living that contributes to their emotional, social, and physiological well-being. We believe that such programs should be available to children during their entire school career.

According to the NISC, there are five primary characteristics of a quality intramural sports program: (1) Participants are limited to students in a specific school; (2) Every student is given an equal opportunity to participate regardless of athletic ability; (3) Students have the opportunity to be involved in the planning, organization, and administration of intramural sports programs; (4) Intramural activities are designed to be voluntary in nature; and (5) While winning and losing are part of the intramural program, the emphasis is on participation and fun.

Most importantly, successful intramural programs are child-centric. The role of adults is minimized.

"It's kids first, all the kids," says Pat Doyle, a leader in the intramural field, regarding what makes a good intramural sports program.

"Besides the obesity epidemic, I can see the decline of intramural sports posing other concerns as well, possibly even more serious," says Kim Overton, a faculty member at North Dakota State University. "Not every student has the opportunity to be a part of a varsity sport, but they should have the opportunity to be part of an organized activity. Students need to have a place where they can feel a sense of belonging and experience the team concept. Intramurals give students an opportunity to participate in an activity they love and to enjoy the social interaction as well."

Intramural programs can be held before and/or after school. However, there are additional benefits besides health and wellness to having the intramural programs before school. As previously mentioned, physical activity is an excellent "learning readiness" tool as it prepares the brain for learning. Research shows exercise enhances academic performance and decreases behavioral problems. Therefore before-school intramural programs may have the most positive impact from an academic perspective. Students will be primed for the classroom after morning intramural programs.

In discussing intramural sports programs, John Byl, professor of physical education at Redeemer University College in Canada and author of *Intramural Recreation: A Step-by-Step Guide to Creating an Effective Program*, says, "Fun, physical activity decreases anxiety and depression and enhances participant feelings of well-being. Research also shows that those involved in physical activity tend to come to class ready to learn, have improved concentration, and have improved overall academic performance."

Intramural sports in schools (K–12) should be an educational adjunct available to *all* students. Emphasis in both physical education classes and intramural programs should be on the physical, mental, and emotional wellness benefits of lifetime participation. In addition, the dangers of limiting one's sports involvement to being a spectator should be continually stressed in these programs.

Competition is an inherent part of sports, but it must be emphasized that one of the greatest competitions any of us will ever face is the challenge of maintaining our own health. With the obesity rate rising, it's clear that too many of us are losing this important contest—most notably today's children.

That's a trend that has to stop. Implementing high-quality physical education and intramural sports programs is an important step in doing just that.

7

SPORTSWORLD NEEDS MORE HUMANISTIC COACHES

We've been conditioned in this country that coaches—from the pros down to our youth leagues—have to adopt a Vince Lombardi-type coaching style; in other words, treat their athletes inhumanely, and motivate them by force and fear. That notion is archaic and inaccurate. Our sports culture needs to evolve from the Dark Ages and transition to more meaningful humanistic coaching styles that enhance the overall experience for athletes while still striving to win games.

Ralph Nader, founder, League of Fans

DEHUMANIZING COACHING STYLES ARE THE RULE, NOT THE EXCEPTION, IN SPORTS TODAY

He treats us all the same—like dogs.

Henry Jordan, former All-Pro defensive tackle for the
Green Bay Packers, on Vince Lombardi

Vince Lombardi's coaching style and the impact it's had on sports in America—from the professional to the youth level—is arguably the worst thing that's happened to sports in this country.

Unfortunately, Lombardi's kick-'em-in-the-butt approach to coaching (autocratic, controlling, screaming, swearing, degrading) has become the model for team sport coaches in this country. We've been conditioned to believe that coaches—at all levels—have to motivate their athletes by force and fear. That notion is antiquated and barbaric.

Yes, there were coaches who used the autocratic coaching style long before Lombardi stalked the Green Bay Packers sideline, but Lombardi stands out as *the* coaching icon in American sports. "Ya wanna win? Then ya gotta coach like Lombardi did," or so the thinking goes.

Undoubtedly, Lombardi was a successful football coach in terms of wins and losses, including winning the first two Super Bowls. His Green Bay Packers teams are legendary. But were his methods the best way to treat human beings? To develop people physically, mentally, emotionally, and spiritually? To make athletes the best players *and* people they could be—in the short term and long term? To promote independent thinking—inside and outside of sports? For building strong relationships?

There are many Lombardi disciples and some of them have won championships. Bobby Knight of Indiana basketball fame is the first one who comes to mind. Pat Summitt of Tennessee women's basketball was for a long time Knight's counterpart on the female side of the game. But there have also been a lot of successful coaches who have used more humane coaching approaches. For example, Don Shula (who was known to talk about "coaching from the heart"), Bill Walsh, John Gagliardi (the winningest coach in college football history), and more recently Tony Dungy in football. In basketball, there's John Wooden, Dean Smith, Stanford's Tara VanDerveer, and today, Brad Stevens, who, before taking the Boston Celtics head coaching job, miraculously took tiny Butler to back-to-back men's Final Fours with a humanistic, people-centered approach to coaching.

The coach has a tremendous influence on an athlete's sports experience—at any level. The leadership style a coach chooses to employ is a major factor in whether that experience will be positive or negative, satisfying or frustrating, fulfilling or miserable.

Over the years, three major objectives for sports have been put forth: (1) Enhance the physical, mental, emotional, and social development of the athlete; (2) Win; and (3) Have fun. Let's call it the sports triad.

The question that needs to be addressed is: "Can you develop the athlete in a holistic manner, treat him or her with dignity and respect, have fun, *and* still win?"

THE OVEREMPHASIS ON WINNING

Make no mistake, winning is important to people at every level of sports, including the youth level. Even in little leagues that don't formally keep score, the kids usually know which team won the game. Often the first question that grandparents ask their grandchildren following a sports event is, "Did you win?"

At a basic level, winning is the purpose of the game. Sports are competitive tests. Thus, winning is certainly a legitimate objective. The challenge is to keep winning in perspective.

There has been some debate over the years about whether or not Vince Lombardi actually said, "Winning isn't everything; it's the only thing." Whether he said it or not, his actions strongly suggested the quote represented the spirit of his coaching ethics.

Joe Ehrmann, author of *InSideOut Coaching*, believes part of the WAAC mentality comes from looking at one's fellow competitors as the enemy.

"We need to look at athletic competition differently," says Ehrmann. "It shouldn't be about winning at all costs. It should be viewed as a mutual quest for excellence."

The key to this type of perspective is to differentiate between striving to win and attempting to win at all costs. A WAAC mentality places values like fairness, justice, and ethics—in essence, sportsmanship—in a secondary role. The WAAC approach is to control and use individual athletes as a means toward winning ball games—the psycho-social ramifications for the athletes as human beings is but a secondary consideration.

It's not just at the professional level where the WAAC mentality proliferates. With the increasing commercialization and professionalization of athletics from the college level down, the emphasis on winning over sports' other objectives has steadily increased as well. Coaches at the lowest levels tend to emulate the coaching styles and behaviors of coaches at the professional level. The sports triad—enhancing the overall development of the athletes, winning, and having fun—mentioned earlier is heavily out of balance in favor of winning, to the point where the WAAC approach to sport dominates at all levels today, including the youth and high school levels.

This mind-set shifts the emphasis in sports from the youth and high school athlete as developing human being to instrument for production of a winning team. With the proliferation of club teams in youth sports, the emphasis on winning has become even greater because club sports organizations are competing for young athletes in the marketplace. A major part of the marketing pitch used by these clubs is built around winning: "Sign up for our club. Our teams have won X league championships, Y state championships, and Z national championships."

"The biggest problem in youth sports today is the win-at-all-cost mentality," says Jim Thompson, founder of the Positive Coaching Alliance (PCA). "It colors everything. Youth sport seems simple but it's very complicated. Part of that revolves around how parents see youth sports. We all want to feel important, like our time on earth is meaningful. For parents, part of that meaning comes from their kids. They are concerned about how successful their kids are in life. But research shows that there's no correlation between success on the Little League field and success in life. In addition, a lot of parents have a belief that says how well my kid does on the field reflects on me as a parent."

THE TWO BASIC COACHING STYLES

What is the best coaching style, given the three objectives that comprise the sports triad—holistic development of the athletes, winning, and fun?

Before we attempt to answer that question, a quick review of the two basic coaching styles is in order. It's important to note that most coaches don't completely fall in one camp or the other. There are many hybrids of the two basic coaching styles: Autocratic (Authoritarian) and Democratic (Humanistic). However, the vast majority of sports coaches today, most notably team sports coaches, fall on the autocratic/authoritarian side of the ledger—even if they believe they don't. Their actions speak differently.

Autocratic/authoritarian coaches have a strong need to control others; they primarily see people as a means to an end: winning. They believe players need to be motivated externally with the lure of rewards or threats of punishment (despite multiple leadership studies that show threats of punishment decrease internal motivation).

Most coaches subscribe to the autocratic leadership style, if for no other reason than it's the style they're most familiar with. It is the type most generally seen by the public as successful and most often emulated by beginning coaches—who if they believe nothing else about coaching, believe you must show up at the first practice with a clipboard, whistle, and a readiness to scream. It is also called the command style or "do as I say" approach to coaching.

Autocratic leadership is manipulative in nature and builds robots more than it does independent thinkers. Authoritarians discourage initiative. This type of leader, also labeled a Theory X leader by psychologist Douglas McGregor (1960), believes players will naturally avoid practice, must be coerced and threatened with punishment, prefer to be constantly directed, and will tend to avoid responsibility. Theory X coaches believe athletes must be forced to complete tasks. They motivate by pressure and fear.

The Theory X style of coaching leadership bears many similarities with the Scientific Management movement in the business world popularized by Frederick Taylor in the early years of the twentieth century. Scientific Management is based on pessimistic assumptions about the nature of man, such that he is lazy and only driven by incentives. Scientific Management principles were quickly adopted by production-oriented businesses looking for robot-humans on assembly lines.

Coaches who employ this style are characterized by a belief in strong discipline, rigidity of rules, and an impersonal attitude toward their athletes. The autocratic coach usually has a strong need to control others and the coaching position satisfies that need.

Autocratic coaches make every attempt to rule the athlete's every move, from practice and games to their private lives, including what they eat and when they sleep. Power is a given; compliance and obedience are expected. Coaches of this type are quick to recognize mistakes and distribute punishments.

As a society, we've come to accept that effective coaches must be autocratic drill sergeants. Think of the sports movies you've seen. Aren't most of the coaches portrayed in these movies Vince Lombardi types? Hollywood has bought into the "coach as drill sergeant" style and fed it back to us. So have sportswriters and broadcasters.

While Theory X coaches tend to see people as merely instruments in the production process, humanistic coaches (Theory Y) are people oriented, prefer collaborative decision making, and believe team performance is strongly related to the satisfaction levels of their players, the sense of internal bonding present within the team, and how much fun the players are having. They believe people are internally motivated when treated humanely and with dignity. Theory Y coaches focus on encouragement and positive motivation tactics. They believe human beings seek out fun, are curious, and naturally want to actualize themselves.

Theory Y leadership stems from the Human Relations School of Organizational Management, which argues that productivity is related to job satisfaction. Theory Y leaders believe that work groups, or teams, that are characterized by a more democratic and humanistic atmosphere will have higher levels of internal motivation, satisfaction, and morale, and as a result, more commitment to the organization or team, and greater productivity than those groups/teams directed by authoritarian leaders/coaches.

Theory Y leaders tend to use a consultative approach. In dealing with team problems, Theory Y coaches typically make decisions through team meetings rather than unilaterally. This contrasts to the Theory X coach's decision-making style of being unilateral, autocratic, and arbitrary.

"I think an interesting way to look at coaching styles is this: If, as a coach, you knew you had to play the last two games of the year without a coach on the bench, how would that change your coaching approach from day one?" asks sports sociologist Jay Coakley.

The German philosopher Johann Wolfgang von Goethe expressed a Theory Y–like philosophy when he said, "If you treat a man as he would be and could be, he will become what he would and could be. If you treat him as he is, he will remain what he is."

The assumption that you need to be a Theory X–type coach in order to be effective is increasingly being questioned today.

In research published in the *International Journal of Sport Communication*, negative tactics, including verbally aggressive language, were found to be less effective in motivating athletes than coaches with a more affirming style.

"This study shows that extra amounts of verbal aggression in the coach-athlete relationship is a negative thing—it's not productive, and many athletes find it to be unacceptable," says Joseph P. Mazer, an assistant professor of communication studies at Clemson University and the lead author of a report on the research.

The key finding from the study is that verbally aggressive language doesn't work as a motivator, even in sports environments where athletes have been conditioned to expect it. Players said coaches who used profanity and other berating language went too far and were de-motivating.

The new study came in the aftermath of the firing of Mike Rice, formerly the men's basketball coach at Rutgers. Rice was fired for his abusive coaching style, including shoving players, throwing balls at players, and verbal assault. Rice's antics were captured on video and soon went viral, pressuring Rutgers's administrators to eventually fire him (after initially coming out in support of him).

A lot of coaches have used methods similar to Rice's through the years—most of them not to that degree, thankfully. Still, their autocratic, aggressive, and occasionally abusive tactics should be unacceptable in this country.

"Coaches, in many ways, are teachers," says Mazer. "And if we hold teachers to high standards with respect to communication, we need to do it for coaches as well."

The Rice situation is certainly ugly, but let's hope the widespread publicity it received causes coaches all across the land to reevaluate their own coaching methods. If they do, and they take positive action, a lot of athletes, of all ages, could be spared the abuse that Rice's players had to endure.

Another way of looking at coaching styles is to examine the Pygmalion Effect. Basically, the Pygmalion Effect states that once an expectation is set, positive or negative, people will act in certain ways that are consistent with that expectation, causing the expectation to come true.

According to ancient legend, Pygmalion was a prince of Cyprus who created an ivory statue of his ideal mate. The result of his work was a beautiful sculpted woman that Pygmalion named Galatea. Pygmalion carried on his life believing that he was destined to spend his life with Galatea and began praying to Venus to bring her to life. Venus granted his prayer.

Today, the Pygmalion Effect, from a leadership perspective, means that the expectations you direct toward a person or group, such as a team, will likely come true.

J. Sterling Livingston, in an article entitled "Pygmalion in Management," in the September/October 1988 *Harvard Business Review*, said, "The way managers treat their subordinates is subtly influenced by what they expect of them."

For coaches, this means that players who receive a lot of praise, encouragement, and communication from a coach, and a sense that the coach believes in them, will tend to aspire and ascend to higher levels of performance. In contrast, players who receive less praise, less communication, and more criticism are likely to feel underappreciated and their performance will level off.

Negativity and demeaning behavior by a coach can result in lower self-esteem and distorted negative self-images on the part of players. But the reverse of that—high expectations, positive reinforcement, open communication—will result in boosts in self-confidence and self-image, along with improved capabilities and performance from players.

"More often than he realizes, the manager [or coach] is Pygmalion," according to Livingston.

Ehrmann, a former NFL player, high school coach, and minister, looks at coaching styles this way:

> We have too many transactional coaches, coaches who use athletes for their own gain and purposes. They use players as tools to meet their personal needs for validation, status, and identity. Transactional coaches are stuck with the old concept of masculinity and believe you need to break kids down and then rebuild them. Their approach is coach first, team second, and players' growth and needs last, if at all. We need more transformational coaches. Transformational coaches are other-centered. They use their coaching platform to nurture and transform players and impart life-changing messages. Their approach is players first, team second, and coach's needs met by meeting the needs of players.

Ehrmann's "transformational" coach clearly falls under the Theory Y style of coaching.

THE THEORY Y COACH IN ACTION

Maybe the best example of the Theory Y coaching style is John Gagliardi. Gagliardi is the former football coach at Division III Saint John's University in Minnesota. He is the winningest coach in college football history, retiring with a lifetime record of 489-138-11 after the 2012 season. In 2003 he won his fourth national championship, to go along with twenty-six conference titles. And he's the anti-Lombardi.

Gagliardi had no film sessions after Monday, no playbooks, no blocking sleds, no tackling leading up to games, and no wind sprints. Nobody got cut. There was no yelling and screaming at players. Gagliardi didn't use a whistle. Practices were limited to ninety minutes. Gagliardi said his practices wouldn't have any resemblance to a boot camp. He had no rules except the Golden Rule. Gagliardi's quarterbacks called the vast majority of the team's plays. If he did send in a play he called it a "suggestion" and the quarterback was free to disregard it. His players loved coming to practice and his graduation record was nearly perfect. Because of the limited physical contact in practice, Gagliardi's teams had fewer injuries and less soreness. As a result, Gagliardi believed his players played with more intensity on Saturdays.

"My whole years I've never had goals, just great expectations," Gagliardi says. A perfect quote from a Theory Y coach who understands the Pygmalion Effect.

Gagliardi is a big believer in having fun with his team. He feels having a sense of humor is a key trait for a coach. "I don't think I could have lasted without a sense of humor," says Gagliardi. "Let's put it this way, there would have been no hope for me to have lasted without humor. Football is made for humor. You have to have a grin now and then on the gridiron. This isn't life and death."

Gagliardi believes the Golden Rule was the only rule he needed.

"I think the key is the Golden Rule," says Gagliardi. "Treat kids the way you'd like to be treated. Coach them how you would like to be coached. We wanted guys to observe the Golden Rule. That will take care of most everything. That was our only rule. Find kids that don't need any other rules besides the Golden Rule. Those who need other rules won't keep them."

On the team's senior speech night a few years back, one senior, linebacker Brandon Novak, described the experience of four years playing for John Gagliardi this way: "Live it up underclassmen, because it goes by fast. It goes by fast, but it'll be the best four years of your life. And once you've played your last game, you'll look back and say, 'This is the greatest place on earth to play football.'"

How can we get more Theory Y coaches, or transformational coaches as Ehrmann calls them?

"You have to do the internal work first," says Ehrmann. "Most coaches fail to do the internal work. That's what my *InsideOut* coaching approach is all about. All lasting and meaningful change starts on the inside. To be a better coach you have to first be a better you. The single best predictor of coaching success is when coaches have made sense of their own lives first. Look at the highs and lows in your life and work to make sense of them.

"Then examine the role sports have played in your life. Coaches have to make sense of the coaching they've received in their lives. Give the coaches you've had in your life grades. How positive was the experience? How negative? What did I learn and what could I have learned?

"Once coaches have done the internal work and developed their coherent life story, integrating the good, the bad, and the ugly, then they can make a clear, conscious choice about what type of coach they want to be.

"It's not just youth and high school coaches either. College and pro coaches can be transformational coaches. Tony Dungy of the Indianapolis Colts was a transformational coach. I did a lot of work with him. He changed the lives of his players.

"It's tough in pro sports because it's the entertainment business. It's a transactional business, quid pro quo. But it's certainly possible to be a transformational coach within that environment.

"John Gagliardi is certainly a transformational coach. He should be a household name in this country for what he's done and how he's done it.

"It doesn't matter if it's sports, business, or politics, you can be a transformational, other-centered leader. Unfortunately, they're too few and far between—in sports and other areas of life."

Ehrmann played for the Baltimore Colts, where he won on the football field, entertained fans, and helped make a lot of money for the team's owner. He was also a me-centered party animal.

Today, Ehrmann is an author and motivational speaker. In recent years, he was also a Theory Y football coach at Gilman High School in Maryland. While his Gilman teams were highly successful on the scoreboard (consistently finishing in the top ten in the Maryland state high school rankings, including a couple of undefeated seasons), Ehrmann stressed a different set of success measures with his players.

In Jeffrey Marx's excellent book, *Season of Life*, about Ehrmann's work, life philosophy, and coaching style, Ehrmann is quoted as telling his players the following:

It's gonna come down to this: What kind of father were you? What kind of husband were you? What kind of coach or teammate were you? What kind of son were you? What kind of brother were you? What kind of friend were you?

Success comes in terms of relationships. Success is measured by the impact you make on other people's lives.

And I think the second criterion is that all of us ought to have some kind of cause, some kind of purpose in our lives that's bigger than our own individual hopes, dreams, wants, and desires. Life's about relationships and having a cause bigger than yourself. Simple as that.

In the book, Ehrmann also stressed measuring yourself against the best *you* can be, not comparing yourself to others.

God gives each person X amount of talent. The question isn't really how many talents you've been given. That's the sovereignty of God. The real question is what you do with the ones you have. Some of us get paralyzed when we feel we don't have "as much as" or [aren't] "as good as" someone else. But the person we really want to honor is the one who maximizes whatever it is he has.

Frosty Westering is another Theory Y coaching legend. He's the all-time NAIA wins leader in college football, with most of those wins coming at Pacific Lutheran. Westering focused on "put-ups" rather than "put-downs" when coaching his players. He built his coaching philosophy around one theme: "Be the coach you would've wanted to play for." (It's interesting to note that both Gagliardi and Westering adopted a version of the Golden Rule as the foundation of their coaching philosophy.)

In his high school and college playing career, he played for traditional, autocratic types of coaches. He didn't enjoy playing under coaches with that leadership style and vowed that he would find another method if he ever became a coach.

"I always said I wanted to coach the way I would've wanted my sons or daughters to be coached," said Westering, who passed away in 2013.

Sports Illustrated, in their 2000 college football preview issue called Westering's program "The Nicest Team in Football."

One of Pacific Lutheran's opponents said of Westering's teams, "When they knock you on your butt, they help you up. They're the classiest team I've played against."

As a former marine, Westering was no softie. He simply preferred utilizing a soul-based approach to coaching rather than an ego-based approach.

Like Ehrmann, he avoided the win-at-all-costs trap by stressing to his players that they were competing against their "best selves," not their opponents.

"The real measure of me is not what I can do in comparison to others but what I can do in comparison to my own best self," says Westering.

One of Westering's players, Steve Ridgway, originally accepted an athletic scholarship from the University of Colorado after turning down Notre Dame. He quickly realized that Colorado's Division I program wasn't for him. He transferred to Pacific Lutheran University (PLU) to play for Westering.

"Frosty Westering showed me how to play the game the right way, what athletics really was all about: that it was bigger than just stepping on the field, making tackles, interceptions, winning games," said Ridgway. "In the time that I was at PLU, Frosty gave me a faith to build my life on, he gave me a hope for the future and a sense that love never fails."

Contrast that style to the style of famous Type X coach Bobby Knight, talking to one of his players here, as quoted from John Feinstein's *A Season on the Brink*:

> You know what you are Daryl [Thomas]? You are the worst f------ pussy I've ever seen play basketball at this school. The absolute worst pussy ever. You have more god---- ability than 95 percent of the players we've had here but you are a pussy from the top of your head to the bottom of your feet. An absolute f------ pussy. That's my assessment of you after three years.

How's that for inspiring leadership?

I'll take Frosty's approach.

LOOKING AT COACHING STYLES FROM A SPORTS TRIAD PERSPECTIVE

What type of boss do you prefer to work for? What type of coach would you want to play for? What type of coach do you want leading your child?

Those are the types of questions we should be asking ourselves in order to help answer which coaching style is best.

Can Theory Y coaches really win on a consistent basis? Well, Gagliardi, Westering, and Ehrmann are all big winners on the scoreboard.

Yes, but those examples are at the high school and small-college levels. Can Theory Y coaches win at the big-time sports level?

As mentioned earlier, winning coaches at the elite college and pro levels, like John Wooden, Dean Smith, Tony Dungy, Don Shula, Bill Walsh, and Brad Stevens, while not pure Theory Y coaches, all would be considered more on the Theory Y side of the ledger. They certainly aren't Theory Y coaches to the extent of Gagliardi, Westering, and Ehrmann.

However, they are much closer to the Theory Y style than the vast majority of big-time college and pro coaches in America today. Call them a hybrid of Theory Y and X, or Theory Z. Theory Z leaders and coaches incorporate pieces of Theory Y and Theory X in their coaching styles. An increase in the number of Theory Z coaches—in addition to growth in the number of Theory Y coaches—would be an important step forward for our society.

Gagliardi believes there's hope for more Theory Y and Theory Z coaches.

"There are fewer authoritarian coaches around," says Gagliardi. "But I think that's true of society in general. There are fewer authoritarian bosses and parents than when I grew up. Back then, everyone thought being the drill sergeant coach was the way to go. I never thought it was. I never responded to being hollered at."

Nevertheless, while there may be fewer of them today, the Theory X coach remains the predominant model in SportsWorld. Increasing the number of Theory Y coaches—or even Theory Z coaches—at all levels will be a challenging culture change process. Owners, big-time intercollegiate athletic directors, the media, and fans have all been conditioned to believe that successful head coaches must be Type X autocratic coaches.

There is a better way.

John Wooden was selected as the greatest coach—of any sport—of all time by *Sporting News*. Wooden reached that level of success by treating players with dignity, rarely raising his voice, and never swearing at his players. He won ten national championships in twelve years at UCLA without resorting to a tyrannical Theory X coaching style.

Wooden believed that athletes are first motivated by the sport itself. His foundational objective was to sustain that original internal motivation, not to falsely create it externally by a reward/punishment system.

"I want the boys to want to come out to practice," Wooden once said. "I want my players to feel the worst punishment I can give them is to deny them practice."

A truly enlightened approach. Still, as a society, we continue to not only accept the Bobby Knights of the world but to view them as what a coach needs to be in order to be successful.

WHY DO WE TOLERATE TYRANNICAL THEORY X COACHES?

It's time to do away with coaching by humiliation and fear. When college coaches choose to coach this way and win, then coaches at all levels feel they have to emulate this behavior. This results in an environment with an enormous rippling effect with harmful social consequences. . . . As parents and citizens, we must stop honoring this primitive and abusive behavior that is tolerated and perpetuated in the name of "winning."

Bill Reichardt, former football player with the University of Iowa and the Green Bay Packers

The great author James Michener, who wrote *Sports in America*, said coaches in the United States get away with forms of discipline that simply wouldn't be tolerated in any other activity.

Frank Deford picks up on that theme. He believes it's time we do something about overbearing youth sports coaches who yell and swear at kids.

"Why, as a society, do we allow such abusive behavior on the part of our youth sports coaches?" asks Deford. "We don't allow teachers to get away with that type of behavior in the classroom, or directors of youth plays, or music teachers. So, why do we let coaches get away with it?"

The continuing dominance of Theory X coaches is simply the result of a vicious cycle.

"Coaches are psychologically frozen," explains the PCA's Thompson, talking about the limited models most beginning coaches rely on. "They tend to coach the way they were coached and by the professional coaches they see on TV."

As parents and fans, we've been conditioned too. But it's time to break the cycle.

Coaching is an area that's ripe for sports reform efforts.

As a society, we need to challenge—at all levels—the conventional thinking that Theory X coaches are the gold standard in coaching, that in order to win, the Lombardi style of coaching—controlling, manipulating, and dehumanizing—must be employed. It's time to demand that our coaches evolve from the archaic, barbaric, autocratic Theory X style toward the more humanistic and positive Theory Z and Theory Y styles.

In particular, we must make a concerted effort to remove tyrannical coaches, those at the far end of the autocratic Theory X continuum, from the coaching ranks—especially at the high school and youth levels.

RECOMMENDATIONS

1. Promote—and Require Whenever Possible— Theory Y–Type Coaching Education Programs

All coaches in this country should take coaching education programs that promote and teach the Theory Y coaching style. Youth sports organizations should demand it. Coaches in our public schools should be required to complete Theory Y coaching education programs because the humanistic coaching style is more conducive to the overall educational mission.

It seems clear that from a holistic perspective—winning, player development, and having fun—the overall needs of athletes—physical, psychological, emotional, and social—are best met under the guidance of a Theory Y coach.

Theory Y coaches educate toward independence and the psycho-social development of the athlete. Athletes under Theory Y leadership have a better chance to become independent decision makers after their playing days are over and the coach is no longer around to run their lives. And given the opportunity, history shows that Theory Y coaches can be just as successful, if not more so, when it comes to winning games and championships.

One of the most impactful things we can do for our sports culture is to focus on transitioning the dominant coaching style from Theory X to Theory Y at the youth and high school levels. By targeting the development of humanistic high school and youth coaches, we can have significant impact, while also influencing young people to become Theory Y coaches when they reach adulthood.

PCA (www.positivecoach.org) is an excellent example of the type of coaching development program that needs to be utilized across the country. PCA is a nonprofit designed to "transform youth sports so sports can transform youth." The organization fights the WAAC mentality that is pervasive in sports, including at the youth level. PCA promotes the development of the whole child through a "double goal" coaching model that emphasizes a humanistic approach to developing young athletes while still striving to win.

PCA founder Jim Thompson promotes a research-based coaching approach centered on the following concepts:

- The ELM Tree of Mastery where "E" stands for effort, "L" stands for learning and constant improvement, and "M" stands for learning to bounce back from mistakes
- Filling the "Emotional Tanks" of players through encouragement and positive reinforcement so they can perform their best and enjoy their sport
- The ROOTS of Honoring the Game: showing respect for the Rules, Opponents, Officials, Teammates, and Self by the way athletes compete.

Thompson says his critics call him anticompetitive. He forcefully denies that claim.

"We're not noncompetitive," insists Thompson. "We like to win, too. The hope I have comes from seeing so many people implement our tools and have success with them. There are so many people who now believe, with all their heart, that the best way to win is to be positive and build kids up."

But Thompson keeps the focus on character development, as does coaching educator Joe Ehrmann.

"Winning's important," says Ehrmann. "We teach to play to win, prepare to win, and plan to win. But winning's a by-product of focusing on developing young men and women of character."

Thompson believes the Vince Lombardi coaching style will continue to be the primary coaching style in America unless we individually and collectively decide to stand up and stop it. In his book *Positive Coaching*, he alludes to the ingrained sports culture that humanistic coaches are up against:

> I am always bemused by commentators who talk about so-and-so, a major college coach, who is so "tough" and shows it by yelling at his players. There's nothing tough about getting negative when things don't go your way. Any three-year-old throwing a temper tantrum is tough in that sense. A truly disciplined coach is one who can provide emotional support to a kid who just blew an "easy" play (easy from the sidelines) that cost a game. He can remain cool while analyzing the situation that contributed to the mistake. Then, at a future practice, he can introduce drills to help the player reduce the likelihood that the same mistake will be repeated. True mental toughness is exhibited by remaining positive in the face of adversity.

There are several other youth sports reformers in the country, in addition to Thompson and Ehrmann, who train youth sports administrators, coaches, and parents and emphasize coaching styles that address the development of the whole athlete, while striving to win and have fun.

Bob Bigelow is a former NBA basketball player turned passionate youth sports reformer whose goal is to take back youth sports from winning-obsessed coaches and parents and give them back to the kids. He's the author of *Just Let the Kids Play: How to Stop Other Adults from Ruining Your Child's Fun and Success in Youth Sports.*

Fred Engh is the founder and director of the National Alliance for Youth Sports (www.nays.org), one of the first organizations created to fight the

WAAC mentality in youth sports. He's the author of *Why Johnny Hates Sports*.

Tom Farrey is an ESPN investigative reporter and the author of *Game On: How the Pressure to Win at All Costs Endangers Youth Sports and What Parents Can Do about It*. He is also the director of the Aspen Institute's Sports and Society program.

Coaches are teachers. We don't tolerate tyrannical teachers in the classroom. It's time we also stop tolerating tyrannical coaches on our playing fields.

2. Start a "Be the Coach You Would've Wanted to Play For" Campaign

When asked about the best coach they've ever played for, athletes usually tell stories about a Theory Y coach they had who believed in them and brought the best out in them, one who was the exception to the Theory X pattern. They describe coaches who were fair, encouraging, gentle but firm, teachers of life lessons who cared about them as people, not just players who could help them win. They talk about coaches who had high expectations for them and helped them live up to those expectations. They talk about staying in touch with these coaches long after their playing days ended.

When asked about the worst coach they played for, it's often a tyrannical Type X coach. Their only fond memory is that they managed to tolerate this coach. They share a badge of honor with teammates with whom they survived the boot camp experiences orchestrated by this coach. But that's about it.

Both Tara VanDerveer, the Hall of Fame women's basketball coach at Stanford University, and Frosty Westering, the tremendously successful football coach at Pacific Lutheran University, have said that their goal upon entering coaching was to be the kind of coach they would have wanted to play for.

What a great concept and foundation for a coaching philosophy! An educational campaign needs to be built around that theme: "Be the kind of coach you would've wanted to play for." In order to be the most impactful, this kind of campaign needs to be a collaborative effort between the NCAA, National Federation of State High School Associations, the National High School Coaches Association, and the various youth sports associations across the country.

Let's call this philosophy the Golden Rule approach to sports coaching.

If every current and future coach in America built their coaching philosophy and style around the question, "What kind of coach would I have wanted to play for?" the number of Theory Y coaches—at all levels—would grow substantially in this country.

It's possible to change one's coaching style this way. VanDerveer's coaching style has definitely evolved over the years. Growing up in Indiana, she followed Bobby Knight and admits that in her early years as a coach she utilized more of a Theory X coaching style. Through the years, however, she's evolved toward the Theory Y end of the continuum, and while she would most accurately be described as a Theory Z coach today—a hybrid of Theory X and Theory Y—she's on the Theory Y side of the ledger at this point in her career.

Thompson ended his book *Positive Coaching* with an apt challenge for coaches:

> First, make your goal to turn every one of your players into a coach so they can pass on to others what you are teaching them about life as well as sports. And finally, never lose sight of what it is you would have wanted in a coach when you were young, and do everything in your power to become the coach that you would have wanted to play for.

3. Conduct More Research in the Area of Coaching Styles

As a country, we need to have more research done on the specific topic of coaching styles in sports. There is a large amount of research—quantitative and qualitative—available on leadership styles in general, and business management styles in particular, but relatively little on coaching styles in the world of sports. Studies are needed that examine the impact of various coaching styles on individual and team performance, athletes' holistic development, levels of satisfaction and enjoyment among players, long-term success and happiness in life, independent decision making of athletes, and even the impact on fan behavior. For example, do tyrannical authoritarian coaches stalking the sidelines incite fan violence at a greater rate than democratic humanistic coaches?

Most importantly, we need more research on the specific impact of coaching styles on the millions of young people that participate in youth and high school sports in our country.

This should be a priority for the sports management and sports studies programs on university and college campuses in the United States.

APPENDIX

Win-Loss Records of Coaches Mentioned in This Chapter

Coach	*W-L-T Record*
Vince Lombardi	96-34-6
Bobby Knight	902-371
Frosty Westering	305-96-7
John Gagliardi	489-138-11
John Wooden	664-162
Dean Smith	879-254
Don Shula	328-156-6
Bill Walsh	92-59-1
Tara VanDerveer	924-207
Tony Dungy	139-69
Pat Summitt	1,098-208
Brad Stevens	166-49 (at Butler)

8

CLEAR ACTIONS NEED TO BE TAKEN TO ENSURE EQUAL OPPORTUNITY IN SPORTS FOR ALL AMERICANS

As a country we've grown lax in our enforcement of Title IX and other laws designed to give all Americans an equal chance to participate in sports. We live in a country in which females and athletes with disabilities continue to be treated unfairly and unjustly in the sports realm. That's unacceptable.

Ralph Nader, founder, League of Fans

THE IMPORTANCE OF TITLE IX

Until Title IX was enacted in 1972, girls and women with an interest in sports were usually told to take a seat in the stands or grab a pom-pom. Sports were the special province of boys and men.

Basically, Title IX was created to prohibit educational programs that receive federal financial assistance from discriminating on the basis of sex. Athletics became the most visible educational program impacted by Title IX.

Regarding athletics, there are three primary areas that determine if an institution is in compliance with Title IX: (1) athletic financial assistance; (2) accommodation of athletic interests and abilities (participation opportunities); and (3) other program areas. It's important to note that determination of compliance is on a program-wide basis within a school, not on a sport-by-sport basis.

In terms of participation opportunities, a three-part test was developed to assess a school's performance in affording potential athletes a chance to participate. The three-part test provides schools with three methods for compliance. Schools achieve compliance by meeting the standard for one of the three tests.

- **Test One—Proportionality**: This first test is based on a comparison of the percent of school enrollment for a gender to the percent of participation in a school's athletic program by that gender.
- **Test Two—Program Expansion**: The second test is designed to judge the school's efforts to expand or increase the number of participants for the historically underrepresented sex—nearly always girls—consistently over time. Usually, schools that achieve compliance through test two have a track record of consistently adding new sports and teams (for example, adding volleyball at the freshman, junior varsity, and varsity levels) for girls, resulting in a significant increase in the number of female participants.
- **Test Three—Full Accommodation**: The third test assesses whether or not a school demonstrates that its sports programs fully accommodate the interests of the underrepresented sex, usually females. In other words, does the school have unmet demand for sports participation opportunities from the underrepresented sex?

Once again, a school is required to meet the standard for *one* of the three tests in order to comply with the three-part test under Title IX.

Title IX of the Education Amendments of 1972 is one of the most important and successful civil rights laws in U.S. history. Yet, to be fully effective at providing equal opportunity, it must be continually and vigilantly defended and protected.

Unfortunately, over forty years after Title IX became law, that vigilance in protecting equal opportunity in sports is often missing. Moreover, there are still people who don't believe that giving girls and women a fair shake in athletics is a good thing. Many of them work to undermine Title IX.

Attempts to roll back Title IX have come from all angles—and at all levels. For example, the George W. Bush administration tried to weaken the third prong of the three-part test and make it easier for colleges and high schools to avoid providing equal opportunities in their athletic programs.

Under the Bush guidelines put in place in 2005, all that schools had to do in order to avoid full compliance with Title IX was to administer an online survey. The flaws in the survey were numerous, but at its core, the online survey strategy was designed to produce results showing a school's female students had no interest in sports beyond what was already offered. Under the Bush plan, if a student didn't respond to the online survey, which is very typical with such surveys, a school could count the lack of response as a lack of interest. In addition, there was no set percentage of respondents needed to determine interest or lack of interest in sports offerings.

USA Today columnist Christine Brennan called the Bush administration's tweaking of Title IX "an assault on the law that opened the playing fields of America to our daughters as well as our sons."

The Bush administration's attack on Title IX demonstrated that while great gains had been made in the area of females in sports, gender equity in American sports was still far from a reality.

Thankfully, then–NCAA president Myles Brand quickly issued an edict disagreeing with the new Bush guidelines. He also told his member schools that they should pay no attention to the Bush guidelines and that the NCAA would not accept surveys for their internal certification purposes.

In April 2010 the Obama administration withdrew the Bush guidelines and restored the original Title IX standards for measuring equity.

In making the announcement, Vice President Joe Biden said: "Making Title IX as strong as possible is a no-brainer. What we're doing here today will better ensure equal opportunity in athletics, and allow women to realize their potential—so this nation can realize its potential."

Well said. That's the true promise of Title IX.

TITLE IX CRITICS ABOUND

As self-evident as the concept of equal opportunity in athletics may seem, there are still a lot of critics and activists out there trying to reverse all the progress the country has made since Title IX was enacted.

Let's look at the arguments of the Title IX critics, one by one:

First, some contend that Title IX represents an illegal quota system. However, the facts say otherwise. Title IX implementation guidelines allow a school to be in compliance with the participation aspect of the law by meeting any one of three criteria, the three-part test outlined above. Of these three, only one is quantitative, the so-called "proportionality test." Every federal appellate court that has considered the validity of the three-part test has upheld it as constitutional. The courts have repeatedly recognized that since schools can be in compliance by meeting the second or third criteria of the three-part test, there is no quota system inherent in Title IX.

Second, other critics of Title IX contend that females simply aren't as interested in sports participation as males and, therefore, don't need as many athletic opportunities. Given the phenomenal increase in sports participation by females since Title IX's enactment, this charge is absurd on its surface. The facts show that female high school athletic participation has increased by approximately 1,000 percent and female college athletic participation has increased by approximately 600 percent since Title IX was enacted.

As Valerie Bonnette, a Title IX consultant, points out, "Women aren't born less interested in sports. Society conditions them." A federal district court put it this way: "Title IX was enacted in order to remedy discrimination that results from stereotyped notions of women's interests and abilities. Interest and ability rarely develop in a vacuum; they evolve as a function of opportunity and experience."

Third, a vociferous group of Title IX opponents say the statute has resulted in fewer sports participation opportunities for males. On the surface, this charge appears to have some merit. The number of men's college wrestling, baseball, gymnastics, and swimming programs is indeed diminishing. However, the decline in these sports is countered by the growth in other sports for males, such as men's soccer, lacrosse, track and field, and basketball. The fact is the overall number of male intercollegiate athletes today is higher than it was in 1981. Loss of male collegiate—and high school—athletic participation opportunities, as a whole, is a myth.

Fourth, critics often argue that football is a moneymaker and its revenues help fund virtually all women's programs. Therefore, men should receive special consideration and have more sports, more scholarships, and bigger budgets. This argument is one of the biggest myths surrounding Title IX. Among NCAA football programs in all competitive divisions, 81 percent spend more than they bring in and contribute nothing to other sports budgets. Even among big-time Division I-A football programs, more than a third are running deficits well in excess of $1 million per year.

It's important to note that only forty-eight athletic programs among the nine hundred–plus NCAA member institutions operate at a profit (at least according to the NCAA's creative accounting methods). Most of the revenue Division I programs bring in is spent on an escalating "arms race" (new facilities, athletic dorms, additional coaches, the latest video equipment, etc.) to keep up with the rivals of a school's football and basketball programs.

In NCAA Division I, the budgets for football and men's basketball consume nearly 75 percent of the total men's athletics operating budget. These supposed "moneymakers" actually churn up money. For these big-time athletic departments, supposedly the most profitable division within college athletics, the average operating deficit is now $4.4 million per year. Universities are forced to subsidize their athletic departments to cover these huge deficits. Academic programs often suffer as a result. Student fees are also regularly increased.

In addition, putting huge amounts of money into football and men's basketball not only increases the likelihood that the institution's athletic department won't meet gender equity requirements, it also increases the chances that *men's* "minor" sports will be dropped.

In reality, the biggest enemies of men's minor sports are football and men's basketball, not women's sports.

"Only by capping these spiraling costs (for football and men's basketball) will institutions be able to grow women's sports programs to comply with Title IX while maintaining existing participation opportunities for men," says a National Coalition for Women and Girls in Education report.

Here's the deal: Division I athletic programs are dropping men's minor sports (sometimes called Olympic sports) because of the football and men's basketball arms race, *not* because of Title IX. In general, Division II and III schools are not dropping men's sports. It's the Division I schools that are dropping men's swimming, wrestling, gymnastics, and baseball programs, often to pay for things such as chartered flights for the men's basketball program or lights for the football team's practice field.

One thing's for sure, football should not receive special treatment when Title IX is considered.

As the Women's Sports Foundation says, "Affording special consideration to football would permit an economic justification for discrimination. This would allow an institution to say, 'We're sorry we can't afford to give your daughter the same opportunity to play sports as your son because football needs more money.'"

A key point to consider is that decisions to drop certain sports (male or female) reflect institutional priorities, not a Title IX mandate. The responsibility of the federal government, through Title IX, is to ensure equal opportunity, not to ensure that particular sports teams are added, dropped, or maintained. It's university athletic directors and their presidents who decide to drop $450,000-a-year sports like wrestling in order to add an artificial turf practice field for the football team. It's these same administrators who give eighty-five scholarships to college football programs when NFL teams can get by with fifty-three players.

As former University of Arizona president Peter Likins (a wrestler in college) said, "We have, as a national society, decided that we prefer to allocate the fair distribution of opportunities for male athletes in a peculiar way, assigning very large numbers of these opportunities to one sport (football) and correspondingly contracting the number of men's sports we can sponsor."

FEMALE STUDENTS STILL TRAIL IN ATHLETIC OPPORTUNITIES

As a result of the opportunities created by Title IX in 1972, approximately three million girls play sports in high school today compared to fewer than three hundred thousand before Title IX.

That's the good news.

The bad news is that according to a National Coalition for Women and Girls in Education report on Title IX, although male and female participation in athletics has grown steadily, female students lag in every measureable category, including participation opportunities, receipt of scholarships, and allocation of operating and recruiting budgets.

In 2007–2008, high school female athletes received only 41 percent of participation opportunities, which is 1.3 million fewer than their male counterparts. On the college side, while female students comprise 54 percent of the college student population, female athletes receive only 45 percent of participation opportunities, 86,305 fewer opportunities than their male counterparts. Moreover, female college athletes receive only 34 percent of sports operating dollars, which is $1.17 billion less than male college athletes receive. Females receive 45 percent of college athletic scholarship dollars, which is $166 million less in scholarship dollars than male college athletes. And females are the recipients of 32 percent of recruiting spending, which is $50 million less than male athletes.

Here's a sobering statistic that will quell some of the excitement regarding the gains girls and women have made in sports since Title IX was enacted in 1972: Since 2004, the gap in the number of sports participation opportunities between males and females has *expanded*, not decreased.

More athletics opportunities have been created for males than females in recent years.

"There are millions of more girls participating in sports today than there were forty years ago," says Donna Lopiano, president of Sports Management Resources and former CEO of the Women's Sports Foundation. "But I thought we'd be further along on this issue. Men's sports are growing faster than women's the last five or six years in terms of opportunities.

"The primary cause is that a lot of schools that should be complying with Title IX are instead funneling all their money into the football and men's basketball arms races instead of addressing gender inequities. The reality is that in recent years men's opportunities are rising faster than women's, and so the gap is growing not narrowing."

THE FOCUS OF TITLE IX SHOULD BE CREATIVELY FINDING MORE OPPORTUNITIES FOR BOTH GENDERS

Title IX is a fair and just law. The issue is really about high schools and colleges doing the right thing and creatively finding ways to equitably distribute opportunities in athletics.

Any changes in Title IX that would lead us back to where we were forty years ago, and once again lessen equal opportunity in athletics, would be a shame. This would also have negative health consequences for half of our population. In this day and age, with obesity and Type II diabetes rates rising rapidly among our young people, we need to take measures that will encourage more participation in sports and other physical activities not less.

That holds for both genders.

The health and social benefits of Title IX for girls and women, and society in general, have been enormous. Research has shown that girls who participate in sports have stronger self-images and lower levels of depression and suicide. They are also less likely to smoke, use illicit drugs, and get pregnant. Additionally, they are more likely to get better grades, graduate from high school, go on to college, and attain high-skill-level occupations in the labor force.

Given these positive outcomes, why would we as a society want to deny equal opportunity in athletics to girls and women?

In the big picture, beyond sports, Title IX is good for our society as a whole, both females *and* males.

The Women's Sports Foundation put it this way:

Title IX is a good law. We need to keep steady on the course of ensuring that our sons and daughters are treated equally in all educational programs and activities, including sports. We also have to protect sports participation opportunities for our sons by making it clear to high school principals and superintendents as well as college presidents that excessive expenditures for one or two priority men's sports and failure to control spending in all sports is unacceptable for educational institutions accorded non profit tax status.

Fortunately, the people who oppose Title IX, while vocal, are in the minority. Close to 82 percent of Americans support Title IX. And the support is broad based with 86 percent of Democrats and 78 percent of Republicans and independents in favor of the law. Moreover, nearly 65 percent strongly support the law while less than 10 percent strongly oppose the landmark legislation.

However, the minority is extremely active, and sadly, many of the most ardent opponents are male athletes, coaches, and sports fans. They mistakenly believe that Title IX has taken away sports opportunities for boys and men. As such, they unfairly attack efforts designed to increase sports opportunities for girls and women.

"Athletics participation is of value to both men and women. Let us leave no one behind because we think sport participation is the right of one gender over another," argued former NCAA president Myles Brand.

OTHER AREAS NEEDING ATTENTION IN ATHLETICS

Despite the progress with Title IX, it's clear from the discussion here that there are several hurdles yet to overcome before we have gender equity in American sports.

We also need to do a better job of increasing opportunities in sports in a few other areas outside the realm of Title IX: (1) disabled athletes; (2) LGBT athletes; and (3) female athletic administrators.

Disabled Athletes

More than fifty million people in the United States have documented disabilities. And these disabled Americans aren't getting anywhere near the same amount of athletic opportunities as their fellow Americans who don't have disabilities.

This fact has many negative ramifications. For example:

- Fifty-six percent of people with disabilities don't engage in any physical activity. That impairs their physical, mental, and emotional health.
- Neither the NCAA nor the National Federation of State High School Athletic Associations officially authorizes any athletic programs for individuals with disabilities.
- According to a Women's Sports Foundation issue paper, the disabled female athlete faces an even tougher situation: Throughout all levels

of sport, women with disabilities are not getting as many opportunities as men with disabilities.

Disabled athletes, most notably in our high schools and colleges, have been pushed to the side, segregated from other athletes, and denied opportunities afforded their classmates, solely on the basis of their disabilities. Incidents of discrimination against disabled athletes have been part of an overarching culture of exclusion and discrimination against individuals with disabilities for far too long.

That said, there have been some positive advancements for disabled athletes in recent years. For example, in 2008, Maryland passed the Fitness and Athletics Equity for Students with Disabilities Act. It has been called a "landmark piece of legislation regarding the inclusion of individuals with disabilities in physical education and athletic programs." The Maryland legislation sets a standard for the rest of the country and is a major step toward providing equal opportunity in athletics for Americans with disabilities. But hurdles remain nationally.

In an article on the Maryland legislation, political activist Terri Lakowski describes why historically the Americans with Disabilities Act and the Individuals with Disabilities in Education and Rehabilitation Act have been ineffective in creating more opportunities for disabled athletes when compared to Title IX and the positive impact it has had on behalf of female athletes.

> Unlike Title IX, which has clear and specific regulations and policy guidelines detailing schools' obligations to provide equitable athletic opportunities and resources to female athletes, specific regulations or guidelines detailing schools' obligations to provide equitable athletic opportunities and resources to athletes with disabilities do not exist under the Rehabilitation Act or the Americans with Disabilities Act. While both statutes clearly prohibit discrimination on the basis of disability, without specific guidelines detailing what specific actions schools must take to ensure athletic and physical activity equity for individuals with disabilities, discrimination and exclusion continues.

However, in January 2013, the Office for Civil Rights (OCR) issued a "Dear Colleague Letter" clarifying schools' obligations to provide extracurricular athletic opportunities for students with disabilities under the Rehabilitation Act of 1973.

The directive applies to K–12 schools as well as colleges and universities. The bottom line of the OCR action is that students with disabilities must be provided opportunities for physical activity and sports equal to those afforded to students without disabilities.

In a press release about the OCR's action, issued by the Inclusive Fitness Coalition, an advocacy organization for disabled athletes, James Rimmer PhD, director of the National Center on Health, Physical Activity, and Disability said, "The OCR guidance is a clear indication that athletics is an extremely important part of our educational system and that youth and young adults with disabilities must be afforded the same opportunities as their non-disabled peers."

The Government Accountability Office has called on the Department of Education to provide resources to assist states and schools in serving students with disabilities in physical activity settings.

"We applaud OCR for its leadership and action, which we hope will pave the way for students with disabilities in sports the same way that Title IX has done for women," said Lakowski, policy chair of the Inclusive Fitness Coalition.

Of course, it takes more than legislation to make a difference in the lives of disabled athletes. The OCR's action was a positive for disabled athletes in the United States but now comes the hard part: enforcing implementation of this mandate.

As has been the case in the quest for gender equity in sports through Title IX, hundreds of sports activists who are focused on improving the plight of disabled athletes are needed. Everyone who cares about equal opportunity in sports must be diligent at the local and/or national level.

"We are ready and eager to work with schools across the country and show them that integrating students with disabilities into school athletic programs is not only feasible, but will greatly enrich the overall athletic experience for all students," said Beverly Vaughn, executive director of the American Association of Adapted Sports Programs.

Skiing filmmaker Kurt Miller (son of famous film director Warren Miller) is one such activist. He devotes a lot of his filmmaking and marketing skills to helping disabled people discover the joy of skiing and becoming active in sports. He has created a nonprofit called Make a Hero that collects and distributes donations for the purpose of making sports more accessible to disabled individuals. He also is making a film called *The Movement* about five disabled skiers in order to stimulate fundraising.

"My job is to build awareness that the need is out there, to educate people to what it means to be disabled, to raise money, and help," says Miller.

A lot of work has been done. A lot is still left to do. Get involved where you can.

LGBT Athletes

LGBT athletes still face an uphill battle when it comes to equal opportunity in sports. Consider that nearly 30 percent of LGBT athletes report being harassed or attacked for sexual orientation or gender expression while participating on a sports team, according to the 2011 Gay, Lesbian, and Straight Education Network's 2011 National School Climate Survey.

The situation isn't any better when it comes to college campuses. The 2012 Campus Pride LGBQT National College Athlete Report revealed that 39 percent of LGBQ athletes have felt harassed because of their sexual identity.

Given these statistics, it's no wonder that most LGBT athletes don't feel comfortable revealing their true identities to coaches and fellow athletes.

LGBT athletes can be discriminated against or marginalized in many ways. Coaches sometimes demand that LGBT athletes keep their identities hidden or try to encourage the athlete to work on changing their sexual orientation. Some teammates try to ostracize LGBT athletes through name-calling, rumor-spreading, or encouraging others to avoid contact with them. In some cases, LGBT athletes are physically threatened or have their property vandalized. Some coaches don't allow LGBT athletes on their teams or give them unfair playing time. The list goes on.

Legally, this issue has all kinds of civil rights ramifications. Morally, it has all kinds of Golden Rule implications.

Two advocacy organizations doing a great job working for acceptance, equal opportunity, and human rights for LGBT athletes are Athlete Ally and You Can Play.

According to Athlete Ally's website, an Athlete Ally is "any person—regardless of sexual orientation or gender identity—who takes a stand against homophobia and transphobia in sports and brings the message of respect, inclusion, and equality to their athletic community. Athlete Allies include competitive and recreational athletes as well as coaches, parents, teachers, league officials, sports fans, other sports participants, and advocates."

Thousands of people have signed the following Athlete Ally pledge:

I pledge to lead my athletic community to respect and welcome all persons, regardless of their perceived or actual sexual orientation, gender identity or gender expression.

Beginning right now, I will do my part to promote the best of athletics by making all players feel respected on and off the field.

Human rights initiatives on the playing field and in locker rooms will make a lot of folks in SportsWorld uncomfortable. They won't want anything to do with LGBT equal opportunity policies.

Writer Jeb Lund put it brilliantly when discussing the mind-set of these people and why it's not worth spending a lot of energy worrying about their uneasiness.

> The big problem of recoiling from change, to spare the people who enjoy things as they are from feeling anxious, is that it privileges people frightened of the future over people with legitimate reason to be frightened over the present. It nurtures and protects ignorance and/or unfamiliarity as something vulnerable and worth preserving, rather than challenging those attitudes and nurturing groups at real risk of violence, social stigma and political impotence. It infantilizes us and lets us believe that hiding under the covers in the dark rather than reaching for the light is the reasonable corrective for a belief in monsters. It takes pains to keep those who enjoy the status quo from enduring any, and in exchange it tells people already marginalized by or ostracized from parts of society that it is for their own good to remain out in the cold.

Moving toward a SportsWorld of equality is unfortunately a slow, painful process. Not everyone wants to go along for the ride. They have to be pushed and pulled, kicking and screaming. Making people face what makes them uncomfortable is part of the process, part of the march to equality on our playing fields and in our locker rooms.

Ultimately, societal progress in any area requires a collective effort.

"This can't just be about groups like You Can Play doing the heavy lifting," says Brian Kitts, cofounder of You Can Play, an organization formed to work toward equality, respect, and safety for all athletes, without regard to sexual orientation. "It has to be a partnership between organizations like ours, professional leagues, professional teams, fans, and gay and straight athletes. And the list goes on from there. This is going to take the same effort as other civil rights causes have in the past, including race and gender issues."

Female Athletic Administrators

Women still lack an equal opportunity to be leaders in college athletic departments. In fact, aspiring female athletic administrators are facing a steep uphill battle. Females occupy 5 of 120 athletic director positions in Division I-A. That's 4 percent at a time when females represent 45 percent of all athletes on college campuses. Moreover, these numbers haven't improved for decades. This fact, in conjunction with a declining trend of women in coaching, makes it clear that women are not being given a fair shot at leadership positions in college athletics.

By comparison, the number of female college presidents has grown significantly over a similar time period. In 1986 10 percent of presidents were women. By 2006, the most recent year for which data are available, 23 percent were women.

RECOMMENDATIONS

Since Title IX came on the scene in 1972, the number of *both* male and female student-athletes has increased. If you believe strongly in equal opportunity as a cornerstone of the American Way, the fact that Title IX was added as an amendment to the Civil Rights Act is cause for celebration.

After all, Title IX isn't just a winner for girls and women. It's a winner for a free, just, and equitable society. As the *New York Times* said in an April 21, 2010, editorial about Title IX, "It is a matter of fairness that transcends sports."

However, we need to continue to do all we can to protect and enforce Title IX. If not, Title IX violations and weak enforcement of the law will undermine our progress toward equal opportunity in sports for all Americans. We need to take strong steps today to ensure that equal opportunity in athletics becomes a reality in this country.

I. Pressure the Department of Education's Office for Civil Rights (OCR) to Aggressively Enforce Title IX and Improve Education Regarding the Law

The fact is, despite impressive gains, more than forty years after Congress passed Title IX, women and girls continue to be denied equal opportunities to participate in athletics based on their gender. Moreover, when given the opportunity to compete, too often they aren't given equitable resources relative to men and boys.

The OCR is the federal agency responsible for enforcing Title IX. In order to ensure equal opportunity in athletics, the OCR needs to vigorously enforce the implementation of Title IX at all levels of education.

More specifically, the OCR must be more proactive in initiating Title IX compliance reviews, and threatening the denial of federal funding when necessary, in order to accelerate compliance with Title IX at the middle school, high school, and college levels.

While the OCR has initiated some compliance reviews through the years, it has not initiated proceedings to withdraw federal funds from a high school or college for noncompliance with Title IX.

Our country's schools and colleges need to see clear repercussions for failing to comply with Title IX. A law can only be optimally effective if it is aggressively enforced.

"Unfortunately, what we see is that many schools are getting away with providing fewer opportunities to girls because they don't do what they're supposed to unless made to," says Neena Chaudry, senior counsel at the National Women's Law Center.

Without an active OCR, the onus has fallen to individuals in terms of fighting for Title IX compliance. Women, and their supporters—male and female—across the country, have been very successful in fighting for female rights in the world of sports by filing civil rights complaints and lawsuits.

"All the plaintiffs in Title IX cases need to be applauded," says Lopiano of Sports Management Resources. "The same goes for all the attorneys that have taken on Title IX cases on a contingency basis. . . . Individuals have to stand up for their rights. In a democratic society, the onus is on individuals. We all have to be prepared to stand up for our rights. That's how our society works."

However, as Americans we shouldn't have to depend solely on complaints and lawsuits to protect our civil rights. The responsibility of the federal government is to ensure equal opportunity through Title IX. To that end, the OCR needs to start doing a better job, and the office needs to be given the resources to do so.

Moreover, the OCR has the responsibility to educate school administrators, coaches, teachers, parents, and athletes about Title IX in order for these key target audiences to effectively spur enforcement.

"The OCR must take affirmative steps to educate school administrators of their obligations under Title IX, and inform coaches, parents and students of their rights to equality," according to the National Coalition for Women and Girls in Education.

The OCR has made some progress in this area in recent years under the Obama administration. But it's just the tip of what needs to be done.

2. Lobby for the High School Athletics Accountability Act (H.R. 458) and the High School Data Transparency Act (H.R. 455)

These bills would require that high schools report basic data on the number of female and male students participating in their athletic programs and the expenditures made for their sports teams. Schools already collect this data and submit it to the National Federation of State High School Associations; however, the numbers are currently not publicly available.

If this information were made available to students, parents, and the general public, it would significantly enhance the ability of interested parties to gauge schools' compliance with Title IX, improve gender equity in sports, and help us, as a country, to better realize the promise of Title IX.

"We need a high school data bill similar to the Equity in Athletics Disclosure Act [EADA] at the college level," says Lopiano. "Title IX lawsuits at the college level have been successful because EADA reports can be easily accessed. They show the raw numbers in college athletics, making it easier to prove discrimination. There are no reporting requirements in high school."

Despite this shortfall, individuals can still move forward without a high school data bill, according to Lopiano. Any advocate for equal opportunity in sports can pick a school district and file an open-records request for data. If it's discovered that girls are being treated unequally in athletics, any individual can file a Title IX complaint. The Women's Sports Foundation website has instructions on how to file a complaint with the Department of Education, Office for Civil Rights. Complaints can be filed anonymously. Once the complaint is filed, the OCR has a specified number of days to begin an investigation.

3. Provide Disabled Americans an Equal Opportunity to Participate in Sports, Including Physical Education, Club, Varsity, and Intramural Sports by Mainstreaming Such Participation to the Fullest Extent Possible and Providing Disability-Specific Programs When Necessary

Pertinent federal and state laws need to be enforced and new laws and policies enacted that require schools (K–12) and colleges to provide equal participation opportunities for individuals with disabilities and specify how such opportunities will be measured.

The OCR's "Dear Colleague Letter," clarifying schools' obligations to provide extracurricular athletics opportunities for students with disabilities under the Rehabilitation Act of 1973, has great potential in this regard. But it will take individual and collective effort to make it happen.

Moreover, the United States Olympic Committee (USOC) and the national sport governing bodies (NGBs), via the Ted Stevens Sports Act, should promote sports opportunities for *all* Americans, including those with disabilities. Unfortunately, the USOC and NGBs are increasingly focusing on elite athletes, including Paralympians, and elite athletic competitions, at the expense of developing and promoting sports opportunities for all Americans.

In addition, "best practice" state laws and education policies should be shared among state legislators. For example, the Maryland Fitness and Athletics Equity for Students with Disabilities Act requires that schools do the following:

- Ensure students with disabilities have equal opportunities to participate in physical education and athletic programs.
- Develop policies and procedures to promote and protect the inclusion of students with disabilities.
- Provide annual reporting to the Maryland State Department of Education detailing their compliance with these requirements.

The Maryland law provides a strong model for legislators in every state.

4. Every State High School Athletics Association Must Develop Nondiscrimination Policies Based on Sexual Orientation and Require That Individual Schools under Their Umbrella Do the Same

Once nondiscrimination policies are in place, public school athletic directors and coaches must be held responsible for promoting a culture of respect in their athletic programs for LGBT athletes. Every school athletic program must provide a safe and welcoming environment for *all* students. Moreover, athletic directors, coaches, and team captains need to make it clear from the first practice of every sport season that homophobia and transphobia will not be tolerated—on and off the fields and courts, including locker rooms.

To support formalized nondiscrimination policies against LGBT athletes, athletic directors should encourage everyone involved with their athletic program to sign the Athlete Ally pledge or something similar.

5. Pass a Law in Every State Similar to California's Landmark AB 1266, Which Allows Transgender Students in Public Schools to Participate Fully in All School Activities, Including Sports Teams That Match Their Gender Identity

Today, the vast majority of states—even those with nondiscrimination policies in place—don't have specific policies that provide the means by which transgender athletes can compete in sports with people of the gender by which they identify. Across the country, transgender students are regularly excluded from physical education classes, sports teams, and locker room facilities.

California's AB 1266 (School Success and Opportunity Act) is the first of its kind in the country. It requires that California public schools respect students' gender identity and makes sure that students can fully participate in all school activities, sports teams, programs, and facilities that match their gender identity.

Once AB 1266 became law in California, the California Interscholastic Federation, which oversees school sports in the state, amended its bylaws to allow athletes to participate in sports based on gender identity.

A similar path needs to be taken in every state across the nation.

9

IT'S TIME TO ESTABLISH A NATIONAL SPORTS COMMISSION

Currently, sports organizations have free rein in the United States. In effect, monopoly is our form of sports regulation. As such, professional sports franchise owners, league commissioners, and other power brokers are the de facto crafters of sports policy in this country—which too often is based on win-at-all-costs (WAAC) and profit-at-all-costs (PAAC) ethos. Therefore, momentous sports reform in this country, given the plethora of recurring scandals and problems, will be extremely difficult without a dramatic change in how this country's overarching sports policy is developed. A National Sports Commission, made up of commissioners representing all sports stakeholders, would be a positive step forward.

Ralph Nader, founder, League of Fans

The United States is one of the few countries in the world that doesn't have a national government-sponsored (at least to a degree) sports commission, sports ministry, or some other entity that plays a significant role in the development of the country's sports policy.

Unlike most countries around the globe, sport policy development and implementation in the United States is almost solely the responsibility of the country's sports power brokers. And these power brokers have a personal vested interest—too often ego based and/or greed based in nature.

The sports policies and operational decisions turned out by these autocratic power brokers usually reflect WAAC and PAAC mentalities and aren't always in the best interests of participants, fans, or the games themselves. Especially troublesome is that these trickle-down policies and mindsets negatively impact high school and youth sports.

As sports reformer Bruce Svare points out, "Too often, the policies that end up directly affecting young athletes are made by individuals who have competing agendas such as the winning of games or commercial interests."

A National Sports Commission would be ideally positioned to develop a national sports policy, a national code of sports ethics, conduct research and analysis on contemporary sports issues, serve as an arbitrator and regulator in clearly defined areas, and be a clearinghouse for all sports stakeholders in the country.

"Without some type of national authority like a sports commission it will be very difficult to have the checks and balances needed to prevent greed from warping sport at its best," according to sports and culture writer Dave Zirin.

EXAMINING THE TYPES OF MODELS THAT DRIVE SPORTS

The Josephson Institute's Character Counts initiative identifies a variety of models of sport. Each model is based on a different perspective of the purpose of athletic competition. As such, each model reflects different priorities and values.

The recreational model is based on the premise that we can all participate in sports to test ourselves, get physical exercise, and have fun.

The educational model is about learning and developing physical skills, as well as life skills such as teamwork, leadership, giving your best effort, and dealing with all outcomes with grace and dignity.

The Olympian model stresses competition for its own sake, dedication to one's sport, and passionately striving for victory. Under the Olympian model, the ultimate (some may say idealistic) goal is the joy of effort and the *pursuit* of victory, not victory itself.

The business model of sports views athletic competition as basically a form of entertainment to generate revenue and positive public relations. This model applies to big-time college sports in addition to professional sports. Unfortunately, it also applies to much of the modern Olympic Games. In the business model, win-at-all-costs and revenue-at-all-costs mentalities dominate.

There's nothing inherently wrong with any of these models of sport, including the business model. However, the problem in the United States is that the business model of sports dominates, and as a result, sports policies and decisions determined by power brokers under the business model filter down to all other levels of sports in America, including high school and youth sports.

AN INTEGRATED SPORTS POLICY FOR THE COUNTRY

You can rest assured that today's sports power brokers don't want to deviate significantly from the status quo.

Therefore, in order to move from greed-based, economic-driven decisions and policies to policies and decisions more consistently based on what's in the best interests of *all* of the nation's sports stakeholders, including fans, taxpayers, and athletes at all levels, a national sports policy, developed and overseen by a National Sports Commission, is needed.

The creation of a National Sports Commission would fill a large vacuum in the United States and provide an important coordinating mechanism for sports in this country. As such, this commission would be charged with developing not only a national sports policy, but a national code of sports ethics as well. The National Sports Commission could also serve as a clearinghouse for all sports stakeholders in the country.

The extent of the commission's oversight role, from the youth level to the professional level, including the Olympic effort, would undoubtedly be a controversial topic. As such, a special committee, authorized by Congress and comprised of sports leaders and stakeholders from all levels of sports, would need to be created to establish the general roles, responsibilities, and parameters of the commission.

The commission would be government authorized but wouldn't necessarily need to be solely a government-funded entity. It could form a variety of strategic alliances with private foundations to help with fundraising and in carrying out its mission.

SPORTS POLICY IN THE UNITED STATES TODAY

The alternative is the system we have today. No government agency is responsible for overseeing sports—at any level—in this country. In effect, a taxpayer-subsidized monopoly is our form of sports regulation, or lack thereof.

In particular, our professional sports leagues have long operated as monopolies, free from the natural regulation of a competitive marketplace—and for the most part, free from any antitrust concerns.

Historically, Congress has stayed far away from the world of sports, especially professional sports, other than granting various antitrust exemptions.

Big-time college sports operate with little restraint under a nonprofit, tax-exempt umbrella given to universities and colleges in this country. This, despite the highly commercialized nature of Division I football and basketball.

Over the past five years or so, we've witnessed a conference realignment frenzy, driven by a cartel called the BCS (Bowl Championship Series). The BCS, made up of six major college conferences, pulled away from the rest of the NCAA Division I-A football leagues and formed its own entity to control the vast majority of football television revenue. While the BCS was formally dissolved after the 2013–2014 season, the BCS conferences—and its commissioners, presidents, and athletic directors—will continue to rule big-time college football and, to a large extent, other sports as well. With the breakup of the Big East conference, it's now the "Big Five" conferences that are running the show, but the same dynamic remains.

In today's college sports scene, universities are jumping from one conference to the next, leaving behind longtime affiliations and rivalries in the quest for more dollars. As a result, fans lose because long-standing traditions and rivalries are broken up. Smaller Division I-A conferences like the Mountain West and Conference USA are left to struggle to survive. And college sport, as a whole, is the loser when a group of schools pulls away from peers based purely on greed. Meanwhile, Congress and the Department of Justice have seen fit to allow these five power conferences to operate as a cartel.

EXISTING SPORT POLICY ORGANIZATIONS

One underfunded, and thus relatively ineffective, sports entity that has a very limited impact on sports policy in this country is the President's Council on Fitness, Sports and Nutrition. The President's Council advises the president about physical activity, fitness, sports, and nutrition through the secretary of health and human services. However, through the years, this group has been small and, to a large extent, powerless. It basically has been a nonentity when it comes to significant policy or regulatory clout of any kind. The council has served mostly a public relations role, especially under the last couple of administrations, during which the council's funding and influence has been cut significantly.

Michelle Obama influenced the relatively recent addition of nutrition to the President Council's mission and her hope was to make the council more active and impactful as part of her fight to reduce the childhood obesity problem in this country. However, the fact remains, the President's Council on Fitness, Sports and Nutrition doesn't have any impactful policy or decision-making responsibilities in the sports world. In an effort to boost the council's funding, influence, and impact, the National Foundation on Fitness, Sports and Nutrition was created in 2010 to promote private sector support of the council. Former congressman and basketball star Tom Mc-Millen is the foundation's founder and chairman. How much impact that effort ultimately has remains to be seen.

In the amateur sports realm, Congress passed the Ted Stevens Olympic and Amateur Sports Act in 1978 to charter the United States Olympic Committee (USOC), as well as National Governing Bodies (NGBs) for each sport. The mission of the USOC and NGBs is to govern American participation in the Olympic movement and promote amateur sports in the United States. In addition, the Ted Stevens Olympic and Amateur Sports Act, through the NGBs and its members, is supposed to protect the opportunity of "any amateur athlete" down to the youth level "to participate in amateur athletic competition." The Stevens Act was also designed to protect American athletes from discrimination in terms of equal opportunity in sports.

According to the USOC's website, the organization seeks to "assist in finding opportunities for every American to participate in sport, regardless of gender, race, age, geography, or physical ability."

In reality, however, the USOC and NGBs do very little in this regard. These organizations focus almost exclusively on a small group of elite-level athletes, not the masses, and only pay cursory attention to the participation model of sports.

Under a National Sports Commission model, the USOC and NGBs could potentially be folded underneath the mission of the commission and be held accountable for promoting sports participation for all Americans—not just top-level athletes—as originally intended by the Stevens Act.

NATIONAL SPORTS COMMISSION CONCEPT HAS BIPARTISAN SUPPORT

The concept of a National Sports Commission has drawn support from both the left and right side of the political spectrum. Conservative Michael Novak has called for a "semipublic, partly governmental and partly private" National Sports Commission with "clearly specified powers of regulation, arbitration, research, and supervision" in the sports realm. Novak proposes a twenty-one-person governing board made up of various sports stakeholders.

Novak's argument for a National Sports Commission is based on what he sees as the unique role of sports as a public interest:

> The positive justification for such a commission is the critical role of sports in the imagination and spirit of the nation. The negative justification is the string of scandals, corrupting practices, and serious grievances now afflicting the disordered and haphazard institutions of sports. Insofar as sports are public services, they have claimed special legal treatment. The logical extension of this conception is special legal oversight. The public interest is substantially involved. . . . Once established by the Congress, such a Commission could be formed by the legitimate election of representatives from the participating categories. This governing board could then choose an executive director for an appropriate term of office.

Sports reformer Bruce Svare, a professor at the University at Albany-SUNY, and former director of the National Institute for Sports Reform (NISR), believes a National Sports Commission needs to be a critical piece of any sports reform initiative.

"The establishment of a National Sports Commission is a must if we are to make any headway in our desire to reform sports to benefit all of our athletes and all of our citizens," says Svare.

Novak's vision of a National Sports Commission focuses primarily on professional sports, while Svare's vision of a National Sports Commission considers amateur sports for the most part. However, there's no reason that a National Sports Commission couldn't be comprehensive in nature, addressing pro and amateur sports to varying degrees. This is especially true when it comes to the development of a national sports policy, which ideally would address multiple levels of sport and a variety of sports issues in this country.

For example, an important role for the commission undoubtedly would be developing policies and objectives around the participation model: sports for all citizens, including the promotion of the health and fitness benefits of lifetime participation in both team and individual sports.

POTENTIAL MODELS: ROLES AND RESPONSIBILITIES FOR THE COMMISSION

There are plenty of examples around the globe of the positive roles national sports commissions and national sports policies can play.

The Canadian Sport Policy was developed by government entities along with numerous private, community, professional, and amateur organizations that influence and benefit from sport in Canada.

The overarching objective leading to the development of Canada's national sport policy was to make the Canadian sport system more effective and inclusive among all stakeholders to achieve the goals of enhanced participation, excellence, capacity, and interaction in sport. One goal of the Canadian Sport Policy is to mitigate instances where professional sport distorts the basic values of sport.

These objectives and goals would certainly be applicable in the United States as well.

Canada also has developed a national Strategy for Ethical Conduct in Sport and established a Canadian Centre for Ethics in Sport.

The European Sports Charter was developed by a committee made up of sport ministers from various European countries. It has many objectives but one is especially pertinent to the subject of commercialization and professionalization abuses in sport: The charter seeks to safeguard sport and its participants from exploitation due to an emphasis on political, commercial, and financial gain. (This objective would be particularly applicable in the United States in the areas of college, high school, and youth sports.) In addition, the charter is linked with the European Code of Sports Ethics.

The Australian Sports Commission (ASC) provides another potential model. The ASC was born with the Australian Sports Commission Act 1989, which laid out the commission's roles and responsibilities.

The ASC administers and funds sport nationally on behalf of the federal government. Its mission is "to enrich the lives of all Australians through sport" and it seeks to achieve a balance among recreational activities, junior-level sport, and elite athletic competition. The ASC also puts a huge emphasis on the participatory model, i.e., getting more Australians active in sports from the youth level through adulthood.

Those outcomes are deeply needed in the United States as well.

The ASC implements sports policy principally through three divisions: Australian Institute for Sport, Community Sport, and Sport Performance and Development. According to the ASC, the commission's "key objectives are to secure an effective national sports system that supports improved participation in quality sport activities by Australians, and to secure excellence in sports performance by Australians."

Other key result areas for the ASC, according to its Strategic Plan 2006–2009, include:

- increased opportunities for children to be physically active
- growth in sports participation at the grassroots level, particularly by indigenous Australians, people with disability, youth, and women

- best-practice management and governance of sport in and through national sporting organizations
- recruitment, retention, and, where appropriate, accreditation of people in the sports sector
- maintaining the Australian Institute of Sports as a world center of excellence for the training and development of elite athletes and coaches
- enhancement of Australia's leadership in the international sports community
- improved economic efficiency in, and commercial return to, the ASC and national sporting organizations
- a drug-free sporting environment
- sustained achievements in high-performance sports by Australian teams and individuals
- increased adoption of the values of fair play, self-improvement, and achievement

RECOMMENDATIONS

1. Create a Special Committee to Determine the Feasibility of, and Parameters for, a National Sports Commission

A Special Committee, authorized by Congress and comprised of sports leaders from all levels of sports (youth to professional), members of Congress, fans, athletes, and other stakeholders, including taxpayer groups, should be created to examine the feasibility, viability, and potential impact of a National Sports Commission. Potential funding mechanisms would be one of the key charges of this Special Committee. The Special Committee would also be charged with developing general roles and responsibilities for the commission as well as budget guidelines.

If the Special Committee determines a National Sports Commission should be created, and Congress authorizes it, National Sports Commissioners could be selected by a panel representing all stakeholder groups: professional owners, college administrators, professional and amateur player groups, youth and high school administrators, fans, umpires and other sports officials, etc. Certain stipulations could be established for commissioners. For example, it could be stated that commissioners could not come from, or go to, the sport industry, in any capacity, for a given period of time (say, three years), to limit influence and bias, as well as enhance the independence of the commission.

Operating funds for a National Sports Commission could come from a combination of government and private sources. In late 2010, the National Foundation on Physical Fitness, Sports and Nutrition Act was passed to help fund the President's Council on Physical Fitness, Sports and Nutrition through the use of resources from the private sector. A similar model could be used to help fund the work of the National Sports Commission. Obviously, policies would need to be developed to avoid bias, conflicts of interest, and unfair influence.

Roles and Responsibilities for a National Sports Commission

There are a variety of roles and responsibilities a National Sports Commission in the United States could fulfill. The following are just a few that should be considered by the special committee:

- **Development of a National Code of Sports Ethics**
  - The Ethics Code would serve as the foundation for the development of a National Sports Policy. The combination of the two could send a powerful message to those involved with sports in the United States that the integrity of sport must be given serious consideration in the development of sports policy—and in operational decision making—from the national level on down to state and local levels.
  - The commission would be a natural advocate for the values, ethics, ideals, traditions, and best practices inherent in sports.
  - The commission's overarching responsibility would be to demand fair, just, and ethical sports programs at all levels.
- **Development of a National Sports Policy**
  - The National Sports Policy would create a new vision for sports in America, one that is driven by more than just commercial concerns and the entertainment ethic. In brief, it would be charged with looking out for the best interests of sport and its stakeholders—all of its stakeholders, not just those with a vested economic interest. It would build from the grassroots level—youth sports, recreational sports, etc.—on up to scholastic and collegiate sports, the Olympic program, and professional sports leagues.

    The current U.S. approach to sports policy in this country is anti-grassroots—flowing from the highest levels down. It's a profit-first and win-at-all-costs approach that trickles down from our pro games to the youth sports level. That approach needs to be thoroughly analyzed and addressed by a National Sports Commission.

- ○ To be effective, a National Sports Policy would need to be extremely inclusive and reflect the input (concerns, needs, wants, expectations, etc.) of all sports stakeholders, at all levels.
- ○ Specific focus areas of a National Sports Policy should include:
  - • Protecting sport from commercialization, professionalization, and politicization abuses in which the basic values of sport are distorted.
  - • Enriching the lives of all Americans through increased sports participation opportunities at the grassroots level.
  - • Balancing the country's emphasis between recreational sport, youth sport, and elite sport.
  - • Increasing the focus on fair play and sportsmanship at all levels of sport.
- • **Research and Analysis on Contemporary Sports Issues**
  - ○ The commission would be a natural clearinghouse for research and analysis on contemporary sports issues. In-house researchers and policy analysts could collect and analyze existing research in a type of "think tank" role. The commission could also conduct its own primary research.
    - • For example, potential research-focus areas could include:
      - ○ Why are young people dropping out of sports for good at such a young age?
      - ○ Why are girls and women suffering a disproportionate number of ACL knee injuries compared to boys and men?
      - ○ Why is the use of performance-enhancing drugs increasing among our young people?
      - ○ What can be done to limit the number of concussions in sports?
      - ○ What are the pros and cons of community-based ownership of professional sports franchises?
      - ○ Why is overall sports participation declining in the United States?
  - ○ The commission could put out white papers, issue backgrounders, position papers, and other documents on key sports issues, e.g., the ramifications of early specialization in a single sport, professionalization and commercialization abuses in youth sports, concussion testing and prevention measures, etc.
- • **Serve as an Arbitrator and Regulator**
  - ○ A National Sports Commission serving as an arbitrator and regulator would be extremely controversial in the United States. However, a range of responsibilities in this area should be examined and

considered by the Special Committee exploring the feasibility of a National Sports Commission.

For example, the National Sports Commission could potentially serve as a "national court of sports arbitration," in a similar fashion to the international Court of Arbitration for Sport (CAS). The CAS uses 150 arbitrators from 55 countries to settle disputes in the world of sports. The CAS's authority as the "Supreme Court of Sports" is well established.

"The CAS has few limitations on what types of cases it can consider: As long as it involves sports, and both parties agree to the arbitration, pretty much any conflict is fair game," according to journalist Brendan I. Koerner.

- **Miscellaneous**
  - If a National Sports Commission is created, Congress should strongly consider folding the USOC, and each sport's NGB, under the commission's jurisdiction. The commission would be responsible for ensuring that the mandate given NGBs via the Ted Stevens Sports Act—promoting broad-based participation in their respective sports—is being followed.
  - The U.S. Anti-Doping Agency, whose mission (to preserve the integrity of competition, inspire true sport, and protect the rights of U.S. athletes) would seem to dovetail nicely with the mission of a National Sports Commission, could also fall under the jurisdiction of the National Sports Commission.

SPORTS MEDIA IS DROPPING THE BALL ON SOCIAL, CULTURAL, AND ECONOMIC ISSUES IN SPORTS

> The sports media are falling dreadfully short when it comes to the in-depth examination of why our major sports problems exist and what can be done to fix them or prevent them. The reporters and editors know this vast gap in their work, of course. Even when they identify key issues, they generally ignore possible remedies, reform efforts, and the people behind them. They're overloading their audiences with sugar—the entertainment and gossipy aspects of spectator sports—and giving them very little in the way of healthy fruits and vegetables—the "whys" and "hows" of our current sports issues.
>
> Ralph Nader, founder, League of Fans

An examination of major contemporary sports issues can't be complete without a look at the relationship between sports organizations and the sports media.

The growth of commercialized sports we've witnessed across the last half century would've been impossible without the symbiotic relationship between the world of sports and the sports media. In particular, television has fueled the explosive growth of both NCAA Division I college athletics and professional sports.

While this growth has had some benefits for fans—e.g., more access to sports events and the deterritorialization of the long-distance fan (fans can now follow their favorite teams across the country and all over the world through a variety of media technology vehicles)—there have also been numerous negative issues that have resulted from the sports media–driven hypercommercialization of sports. These negatives have impacted not only pro and big-time college sports but have filtered all the way down to the high school and youth sports levels—where sports have increasingly become distorted due to professionalization driven by WAAC and PAAC mentalities.

From a journalistic ethics perspective, the sports media has the corporate social responsibility to give us more than game coverage, trade rumors, and injury reports from our big-time sports leagues. Sports media organizations, and individual journalists, need to do a better job of holding those with power and influence in sports accountable.

Take the gender equity issue in sports today as but one example.

"There needs to be more attention paid to the data," says Donna Lopiano, former CEO of the Women's Sports Foundation. "The media should be writing about the data on Title IX compliance and calling out those institutions not complying with the law. The Women's Sports Foundation and other advocacy organizations have been doing a good job preparing reports on the inequities. The transparency of the facts is crucial. That can ignite more media stories.

"When those not in compliance with Title IX get some bad press, that's how institutions change. Schools not in compliance with Title IX need to be embarrassed by bad press and lawsuits."

As a whole—and there definitely are exceptions—the sports media too often simply identifies the symptoms of problems and then stops. Rarely do sports journalists and their editors dig for root causes or examine important sports issues from a holistic perspective, including social, educational, economic, safety, and health angles. And they don't ask questions like, "Is sport, as presently constructed in this country, meeting the needs of participants, spectators, taxpayers, and families?" There's virtually no examination of the core sports systems and models at work. For the most part, they're taken for granted.

Where's the deeper discussion on the challenges in overcoming a given problem in the world of sports? Where's the well-rounded examination of an important sports issue, utilizing financial, education, and legal reporters within a given news organization? Where are the features on groups and individuals working in the trenches to address contemporary sports problems in order to make the world of sports better for all stakeholders? Where are the town hall–like discussions and strong penetrating interviews?

"Increasingly broadcasters have become essentially partners with the sports organizations they're covering because the companies these broadcasters work for are also presenting the games," says sports journalist Robert Lipsyte. "We've had some wonderful investigative exposés in sports, especially with the recent scandals in college sports, but what they've basically all said is, 'We've located the cancer, just cut out the tumor and we'll be fine,' rather than saying, 'The whole system is corrupt.'

"Look at the Penn State situation. The feeling in the sports media seems to be: 'Just get rid of everyone and the thing will be whole again.' But it's the system that's the problem in college sports. The way individual football players have been treated—one-year contracts, no protection from physical injuries, etc.—it's terrible.

"Actually, some of the best work on sports today is being done by serious nonsports people, who are beginning to look harder at the system and its corrupting institutions."

As Daniel Libit effectively pointed out in a September/October 2011 *Columbia Journalism Review* article entitled "The Scandal Beat," sports journalists are doing okay examining who's breaking the rules but have been poor when it comes to analyzing whether the rules and the underlying system make any sense to start with.

The bottom line is the sports media is falling woefully short when it comes to in-depth examinations as to why our major sports problems exist and what can be done to fix them or prevent them.

That needs to change. There certainly are plenty of critical sports issues to examine, as this book can attest.

Basically, it comes down to this: Are sports media reporters, editors, and executives going to continue to be about commercial entertainment sports coverage and putting profit-at-all-costs objectives above their journalistic and corporate responsibility ethos or will they aspire to something higher?

THE SYMBIOSIS OF SPORTS MEDIA AND COMMERCIAL SPORTS THROUGH THE YEARS

> Television buys sports. . . . Television tells sports what to do. It *is* sports and it runs them the way it does most other things; more flamboyantly than honestly.
>
> Leonard Shecter, sports journalist

The mass media provides the financial foundation that drives commercial-ized sport. That has been the case for decades now.

However, the sports media, most notably television, is more powerful than ever. As an example, approximately 75 percent of NFL revenues come from rights fees today, up from 45 percent in 1979.

Before the early 1950s there was no television and prior to the 1920s there was no radio. Before radio, media coverage of sports was strictly of the print variety. But from the beginning, sports organizations have de-pended on the sports media for free publicity. And the sports media have long depended on sports to boost readership, listenership, viewership—and, of course, to sell advertisements.

Newspapers love sports and their sports sections are in effect free advertising pages for big-time commercial sports entities. According to sports-studies professor Ronald Woods, "Most major newspapers in North America devote more space to sport than any other topic, including busi-ness, politics, and world news."

Nevertheless, while newspapers and radio have long been linked with commercial sport, television and sport represent the true symbiosis.

Sport and television have been growing together for nearly sixty years. From television's early days, sporting events were seen by television execu-tives as providing perfect content for the networks. At the same time, pro sports franchises and major college athletic programs quickly saw television as an excellent way to build conference and team recognition (and of course revenues as well) and to grow their audiences beyond their previously lim-ited geographic areas.

Garry Whannel, director of the Centre for International Media Analysis at the University of Bedfordshire (U.K.), summarizes the unique symbiosis between sports and television by saying that "in a world dominated by and in many ways defined by media imagery, it is in no small part sport that drives television—it is one of the primary forms pushing the commodifica-tion of television . . . [and] the only viable pay-per-view form of television."

By 2000 twenty-nine North American professional teams were wholly or partially owned by media corporations. Rupert Murdoch is a leading example. He has called sports "the cornerstone of our worldwide broad-casting efforts." Murdoch has created a global sports media empire and has publicly committed to commercially exploiting sport for the benefit of his television business. He has invested billions in sports in the United States alone. *Sporting News* named him the seventh most powerful person in sports during the twentieth century. And while he has divested some sports holdings during the last decade, that power and influence remained during the first decade of the twenty-first century. In 2007 *Business Week* named him the tenth most influential person in the world of sports.

More recently, Murdoch and his Fox network, along with NBC, ESPN, CBS, and DirecTV agreed to help NFL owners underwrite the 2011 NFL lockout and provide the owners money in the event there wasn't a 2011 NFL season. The NFL players challenged that arrangement in court but the challenge became moot once the owners and players reached an agreement and the lockout ended.

The growth of sports on television in the United States has been nothing short of phenomenal. In the early 1980s, about twelve hundred hours of televised sports were broadcast annually. Today, more than sixty thousand hours of sports coverage are televised every year. That coverage is spread across four major free-to-air networks as well as numerous pay-TV platforms, including cable, pay-per-view, satellite television, and various local sports cable and digital channels. As networks look for more sports programming they've turned to high school and youth sports programming (e.g., the Little League World Series), which, in turn, has created a whole new set of issues.

This sports television explosion is far from solely an American phenomenon. For example, the French Centre for the Law and Economics of Sports says the amount of televised sports on French television multiplied more than 140 times between 1968 and 1999.

Internationally, the World Cup final soccer game is the most-watched worldwide sports event every four years, drawing more than twice as many viewers as any other program during that given year. The Super Bowl is typically a distant second.

The 2008 Beijing Olympics were watched by 4.7 billion viewers, which meant more than two out of three people worldwide turned in for at least some part of the Olympic telecasts. That viewership was 20 percent larger than the Olympics drew only four years earlier. In the United States, 215 million Americans watched the Beijing Olympics.

Four years later, more than 219.4 million Americans watched the 2012 Summer Olympics in London, making those games the most-watched event ever in U.S. TV history, according to Nielsen. The 2012 Olympics drew more than four million more U.S. viewers than the 2008 Beijing games. Worldwide viewership was approximately 4.8 billion viewers in 2012.

The tremendous size and growth of today's big-time commercial sports industry in America (including pro sports leagues and NCAA Division I football and men's basketball) is almost completely attributable to television-rights deals. Moreover, the escalation in both pro sports franchise revenues and player salaries (along with the market values of those pro franchises) is directly correlated to the rise in television-rights fees. (This booming growth in revenues for NCAA Division I college football and basketball programs makes the fact that college athletes in these sports aren't allowed a piece of the pie even more egregious.)

According to sports sociologist George Sage, if television ever withdrew its money from sports, the entire pro sports structure in its present form would simply collapse.

THE SPORTS MEDIA HAS CHANGED THE ESSENCE OF OUR GAMES

> Now think about this: Capitalist corporations sponsor nearly 100 percent of all sports programming in the media, and their goals are to create consumers loyal to capitalism and generate profits for corporations and their shareholders. However, we seldom question how this influences *what* we see in sports coverage, *what* we hear in commentaries, and *what* we do *not* read, see, and hear as we consume media sports.
>
> Jay Coakley, sports sociologist

Due to the money television networks have invested in sports, they've been able to influence the leagues in many ways, including modifying the rules of the games.

Television executives aren't interested (at least primarily) in the purity of sport—or the rules, traditions, and values of our games, for that matter. They simply look for ways to make sports more profitable. If that means modifying how the games are played, where they're played, and when, so be it.

For example, it is standard in today's sports television-rights agreements to have a provision allowing for preset television time-outs during games in order for television partners to air as many commercials as possible. (This is a nuisance not only to television viewers but also to those attending the games. These fans have paid outlandish ticket prices for the privilege of sitting through mind-numbing TV time-outs. And, of course, this break in the action means more advertisements can be blared through the giant scoreboard systems in our stadiums and arenas—providing another revenue opportunity for the home team.)

Television networks now are the de facto determiners of schedules and starting times for our sports. Schedules and start times are manipulated in order to maximize ratings and, thus, advertising revenue. It doesn't matter if baseball play-off games end at 1 a.m. on the East Coast. It doesn't matter if young sports fans are in bed and not watching the climatic conclusions to these play-off games, thus jeopardizing the long-term future of the game. It's all about maximizing dollars today, not the best interests of the sport or its stakeholders.

The designated hitter (DH) in baseball can be traced to television pressure to get more home runs and scoring in the game in a quest to lure more fringe fans (and, yes, boost ratings and advertising revenue). Television power brokers didn't consider what the DH might due to the essence of the game of baseball, including strategic decision making.

Traveling and palming violations have gone the way of the dinosaur in the NBA because television executives found them to be annoying hindrances to exciting offensive plays like slam dunks.

These are just some of many examples, throughout sports, of television's influence driving rule changes to enhance offensive play and limit defensive effectiveness.

Television executives have also pushed for longer regular seasons and extended play-offs because they love the programming content sports provides. The more the merrier in their minds. However, for the athletes the result is more games where athletes aren't at their peak due to fatigue and injuries. For the fans, regular-season games become devalued and the entire regular season is cheapened as more and more teams are allowed into the play-offs.

Even sports like golf and tennis have been altered due to the power of television. Match play in golf has almost disappeared from the golf landscape due to the fact TV doesn't appreciate its unpredictability, which makes it harder for them to schedule programming. Tennis was pushed by TV to adopt set tiebreakers because it allowed television executives to better predict the length of tennis matches, again for programming purposes.

Recently, the college sports landscape has been significantly altered due to conference realignment, which has been driven completely by—you guessed it—the chase for more television revenue. As a result, longtime traditional rivals have been split up and schools are being placed in conferences that make no geographic sense—increasing the travel burden on college athletes (in all sports a conference sponsors, not just football) and hindering their chances to be students as well as athletes while they're on campus.

Perhaps most disturbingly, the values of commercialized sports and the sports media have filtered all the way down to the high school and youth sports levels. How does it make any rational sense to have high school basketball and Little League baseball games televised nationally? Those decisions certainly weren't made in the best interests of the young people involved.

The influence of the sports media has swung the pendulum toward sport as entertainment—at every level—and away from sport as cultural practice (e.g., form of exercise, educational activity, and childhood development tool).

CORPORATE RESPONSIBILITY AND THE SPORTS MEDIA

> The corporation must not only benefit those who create it, it must benefit those who permit it.
>
> Norman E. Bowie, professor emeritus of strategic management and
> philosophy at the University of Minnesota

The role of the sports media in society comes down to this question, "Does the sports media have a responsibility to society, sport, and its stakeholders, beyond simply seeking profit at all costs?"

Journalism watchdogs and academics are united around a "yes" answer to that question.

"Sports media should be chronicling *every* aspect of the games—on and off the field, including social issues as they play out in sports," says Kelly McBride, senior faculty in ethics, reporting, and writing for the Poynter Institute and a key player on the Poynter Review Project, an independent examination and analysis of ESPN's media outlets. "The media should certainly hold the powerful accountable. . . .

"The sports media has an obligation to cover all of the world of sports, including money, power, and the major social issues. You certainly have to be able to cover these issues as well [as the games themselves] to call yourself a good sports journalist or sports journalism organization."

So, why isn't the sports media doing a better job with this responsibility?

"I think they'd like to be doing a better job in this regard," says University of Florida professor Ted Spiker, who teaches a sports, media, and society course. "The problem is sports media companies are under increasing pressure for ratings and page views. The allure of entertainment 'quick hits' too often gets in the way."

Basically, it's simply easier to feed sports media consumers more game coverage, trade rumors, injury reports, and player scandals than it is in-depth discussion and analysis of the critical social, cultural, and economic issues of the day in sports, including examining the foundational sports systems that lead to the scandals.

In-depth issue exposés, analyses, features, and documentaries take more time and effort than basic game coverage and analysis. For example, Charles Robinson reportedly spent eleven months on the University of Miami football scandal story for Yahoo! Sports. That's a significant commitment to true journalism that a lot of organizations—print, radio, and television—aren't willing to make.

"There's not enough time or bodies to produce this type of work on a regular basis," says Malcolm Moran, director of the John Curley Center for Sports Journalism. "The challenge is at a point, given the economics of the industry, where it takes a lot of resources to do that reporting."

There may be a lot of truth in that statement for the sagging print industry but sports television is doing just fine financially and could easily devote more resources toward sociocultural sports issues. No matter what, it comes down to priorities, given the large "news hole" that sports is given in print, radio, and television media. There is certainly room for reporting on the sociocultural issues of sports.

"In the sense of the conglomeratization of sports, the perceived agents of journalism—ESPN, Fox, NBC—have become so involved with the leagues that it's hard to believe you can get honest journalism from them," says Lipsyte. "The systemic criticism needed in sports is not going to happen as long as the same people that broadcast the games also report on the games."

SPORTS MEDIA IDENTIFIES PROBLEMS
BUT THEN STOPS

In recent years, some sports journalists and outlets have been doing a pretty good job identifying important contemporary sports issues and describing the problems involved (e.g., concussions in sports—albeit belatedly). Moreover, they've done a number of excellent investigative reports and opened the window on some major scandals, most notably in big-time college athletics. (As previously mentioned, as Exhibit I, see Charles Robinson's excellent work on the University of Miami football scandal.) Taylor Branch's in-depth article on college sports in *The Atlantic* was superb. It's interesting to note that some of the best work in sports has been done by nonsports journalists, including Branch.

There are several other journalists doing good ongoing work on important current issues (e.g., Dan Wetzel of Yahoo! has been a regular critic of the BCS system in big-time college football; likewise with ESPN's Tom Farrey on youth sports. Dave Zirin is one of the more enduring and wide-ranging critical sportswriters we have when it comes to analyzing contemporary sports issues, and Patrick Hruby is doing excellent work for *SportsOnEarth*). There are also a few sports media companies that are doing a commendable job of watchdog sports journalism. (*USA Today* comes to mind for its occasional work on minority hiring in sports, as well as on the issue of college sports finances. *Sports Illustrated* will occasionally have a solid piece in this area.)

However, as a whole, the sports media too often simply identifies the symptoms of problems and then stops.

Libit touches on the primary problem with today's sports media: a lack of depth on critical sports issues.

"The reporting, intentionally or not, promotes the idea that the corruption that plagues the NCAA is the problem, rather than merely a symptom of a system that is fundamentally broken," writes Libit. "The Scandal Beat, with its drama and spectacular falls from grace, is much less adept at managing the next step: a robust discussion, prominently and persistently conducted, of why these scandals keep happening and what can be done to prevent them."

Libit was writing about the sports media's coverage of the problems and abuses in college sports, but the same could be said regarding the sports media and many of the other problems, issues, and abuses in sports.

A key "How?" question, "How should we respond as a society to these problems?" is virtually ignored by the sports media.

In Libit's discussions with sportswriters, he found that most agreed with his thesis: Today's sports journalists rarely get at the underlying problems.

For example, Rick Telander, a sports columnist for the *Chicago Sun-Times*, calls the rules violators in college sports the "crumbs of the problem."

"The big muffin is right in front of us every day," said Telander. "We know it and accept it, so that's where all the craziness starts. We all accept the Big Lie, so we are dazzled and amazed by the little lies. I have found that completely self-defeating and really it hasn't changed."

Acceptance of the Big Lie, when looking at most sports issues, is the core reason why our sports media fails when it comes to providing serious reporting, reflection, and analysis on the sports issues of the day.

"In this way, the Scandal Beat sets its own trap," writes Libit. "It produces important stories that fit into a celebrated tradition of muckraking and watchdog reporting. They are the kinds of stories that win prizes and generate traffic. . . . The result is straightforward coverage of the NCAA and its rules—and the inevitable violations of those rules—rather than coverage that challenges the validity of the rules themselves, and the system that upholds them."

As good as Robinson's work was on the University of Miami scandal, the corrupt NCAA system, the very foundational model of college sports that led to the scandal, was basically taken as a given and left alone.

It appears that what we're dealing with here is a classic case of hegemony. Robert Lipsyte, in his groundbreaking book *SportsWorld: An American Dreamland*, was one of the first to identify the hegemonic forces at work in sports in this country.

"Hegemony literally means dominance," wrote sports sociologist George Sage in his book *Power and Ideology in American Sport*. "But more broadly it describes a sociopolitical situation in which one way of thought and life is dominant and is diffused throughout various social institutions [including media] and cultural practices."

The dominant ideology of big-time commercial sport is diffused through corporate entities like the sports media. To a large degree, employees—including sports journalists—have bought into the existing sports systems and models in this country. It's what they're familiar and comfortable with.

In effect, most sports journalists are drinking the grape Kool-Aid, and any suggestion that it's not the rule breakers that are the most fundamental problem but the sports model itself is met with swift rejection.

The majority of sports journalists believe they have too much invested in the existing system—either economically, psychologically, or both—to say, "Wait a minute, let's look at the core of this issue, or this particular problem, and see if some changes need to be made at the foundation of SportsWorld, with the systems and models that are in place."

Author and historian T. R. Bates once wrote that power is achieved and maintained via "leadership based on the consent of the led, a consent which is secured by the diffusion and popularization of the world view."

In the case of sports in America, the "world view" is one that is shared by the power brokers in both the sports and media industries—"winning is everything; profit at all costs, etc." And consent regarding this worldview is too often given—albeit often unwittingly—by sports journalists.

The challenge for those of us who care about sports (fans, participants of all stripes and abilities, and any activist/reformist-minded journalists) is to identify what's going on, why it's going on, and then focus on the "how"— how can we effectively work to challenge the existing "worldview"?

RECOMMENDATIONS

Hegemony can be, and has been, successfully challenged throughout history. Dominant ideology doesn't just passively exist; it has to be continually reinforced and defended. This becomes more difficult for the power brokers when it is constantly challenged and resisted. Throughout American history, the media has played a critical role in this regard.

History has shown that hegemony and compliance are never assured. Many athletes, and other sports stakeholders, have successfully resisted hegemonic forces in sport. Journalist Lester Rodney, athlete Jackie Robinson, and executive/owner Branch Rickey come immediately to mind for their roles in integrating baseball, but there are numerous other examples at both the national and local levels.

Big Sport can be resisted and, ultimately changed. We don't have to be hopeless saps to the dominant sports ideology as promulgated on a regular basis by the traditional sports media. It's time to engage in the struggle.

It's worth the effort.

1. Demand That Sports Media Organizations Establish a "Sports Issues and Reform" Beat

All sports media organizations, whether print, radio, television, or Internet based, should establish a sports issues/reform beat to take a deeper look at critical contemporary sports issues and the various efforts by individuals and groups in society to address those issues. Ideally, they would also examine the root causes of the issues in question and the models and systems that propagate them.

This type of work is a core value of journalism in America. It's part of the "journalistic duty" of every media organization, however they may define it.

The sports issues/reform beat could include a weekly sports issues section in newspapers, along with weekly sports issues shows (like ESPN's *Outside the Lines*) on radio and television.

These types of investigative articles and shows need to go beyond *Outside the Lines*'s examination of the "What?" and "Why?" of the issues, to the "How?" How can the existing structures, systems, and models of sports be modified or scrapped for the betterment of all sports stakeholders?

Sports talk shows could be developed in this realm (Dave Zirin's *Edge of Sports* on SiriusXM radio is an example). These shows/segments could discuss the "issue of the day/week" with various outside perspectives represented beyond those of the dominant ideology in sports.

As Ralph Nader suggests, we, as sports stakeholders, concerned about the health of sports as an important cultural practice in our society, must demand that the sports media feeds us more fruits and vegetables and a little less sugar.

2. Every Sports Media Organization Should Add an Ombudsman to Extend the Voices of Fans and Other Sports Stakeholders and to Investigate Their Complaints

The ombudsman role has served society well through the years. Unfortunately, the ombudsman function in the media industry has become increasingly scarce in recent years, as the corporate quest for profit has usurped every other objective, including journalism ethics.

The ombudsman function plays an important role in the halls of power by representing voices that are traditionally largely underrepresented. The sports ombudsman could advocate for more avenues to hear from fans and recreational athletes, including letters to the editor (which have become rare in American sports sections), op-ed columns from community sports voices that are seldom heard from in our "spectator sports" sections, and sports-forum-type radio and television shows that have representatives from all stakeholder groups.

A positive move in this direction was ESPN's hiring of Robert Lipsyte as ombudsman. His background makes him ideal for this role.

3. The Sports Media Should Cover All Aspects of Sports, Not Just Highly Commercialized Spectator Sports

As Kelly McBride of the Poynter Institute has pointed out, in order to call yourself a sports journalist, or sports journalism organization, you need to cover the social, cultural, and economic issues of all aspects of sports, not just provide game coverage and related analysis in the spectator sports realm.

That includes spending more time (it's virtually nonexistent today) on "Sports for All" topics. This would require examining participatory and community sports events, topics, and issues in addition to covering solely spectator sporting events. And it requires more than a cursory look at the issues. Major issues, such as the abuses in youth sports, and the decline of physical education and intramural sports in our schools—especially in relation to our childhood obesity epidemic—demand in-depth investigations.

4. Utilize the Tools of the Internet to Challenge Big Sport

The "democracy of the Internet," and its growth and technological developments, is one of the greatest things ever to happen to the oppressed in society. The social media revolution (Facebook, Twitter, blogs, and alternative "newspapers") has helped facilitate uprisings against dominant political and corporate ideologies across the globe. The Internet is not only a great communications tool but can be an excellent organizing tool as well—in all areas, including sport. In effect, it has the potential to make activist sports journalists of us all.

If the traditional sports media remains entrenched against change in the world of sport, then oppressed and frustrated groups and individuals in SportsWorld need to turn to the Internet in order to galvanize against the power brokers in sport. Fans, recreational athletes, taxpayers, and others can utilize social media, independent reporting, organizing and petitioning tools, and blogging to make a difference by addressing the dominant commercial sports ideology head-on and forcing changes in the areas of both sports and sports coverage.

11

CALLING ALL POTENTIAL SPORTS REFORMERS

The number of important issues and abuses in sports has never been greater. Win-at-all-costs and profit-at-all-costs policies and decisions are warping the original intent of sports and increasingly sapping the joy from them. We need to come together and work to take our sports back from those who view them as just another way to make a lot of bucks.

Ralph Nader, founder, League of Fans

There are a lot of things the average fan or participant out there can do to make sports more fair and just. We have to stop letting the big honchos of sports set the agenda for the system. We need to make our own demands regarding how sports can be. I think there are three basic ways for people to get involved: (1) Get involved with organizations that are working to make the sports experience better; (2) Get loud and vocal about the sports issues that bother you, locally and nationally; and (3) Pressure lawmakers to step in and be accountable. We all have every legal, moral, and ethical right to be heard on these issues.

Dave Zirin, activist sports journalist

When I was interviewing Joe Ehrmann, he gave the best answer I've ever heard to the question, "What should sports be all about?" Ehrmann is a former NFL football player, coach, and minister. He now heads up an organization called Coach for America.

UNIVERSITY OF SAN FRANCISCO
LIBRARY

Here's his answer:

Sports should be about the social, moral, and ethical development of young people. It's about character if done the right way. However, one of the great myths is that sports build character. That's certainly not true in the win-at-all-costs world of sports in our culture.

Life is a team sport. Nobody goes through this world alone. It's about a commitment to relationships and treating people with respect and dignity as you work on a common cause. That's what team sports can teach at their best. Team sports are about a set of relationships working on a common cause.

Sports should be about creating good citizens and change agents. Sports should be a means to an end. Today, sports have become an end in themselves.

I also believe sports should be cocurricular, not extracurricular. Every coach has the last classroom of the day. Coaches should be teachers and act like teachers. In a math class, we would never tolerate a teacher swearing, yelling at kids, or shaming a kid because they got a math equation wrong. Why do we allow that in sports?

We also need to look at athletic competition differently. It shouldn't be about winning at all costs. It should be viewed as a mutual quest for excellence.

Finally, sports should be about the health and well-being of every participant. We need to get more kids involved and create more alternatives so every kid can participate in team sports.

Wow. I think Ehrmann pretty much nailed it. Sure, professional sports is a different animal than youth, high school, and college sports, but I think Ehrmann did a nice job capturing the essence of sports, the spirit of sports, if you will, at all levels. About the only change I'd make is to include "adults" in the last paragraph of that answer along with "kids."

To get to the point where that spirit drives our policy making and decision making in sports, we'll need to overcome something called Sports Syndrome.

A BIG CHALLENGE: OVERCOMING SPORTS SYNDROME

A long habit of not thinking a thing wrong gives it a superficial appearance of right.

Thomas Paine

Sports, at all levels, have become so commercialized and professionalized—and thus warped to a large degree—that those who love sports need to become engaged beyond being simply diehard fans and/or active participants.

We can't just blindly sanctify sports anymore and look at sports with the romantic eye of our youth. Those of us who are passionate about sports—but hate what they are becoming—need to join together and reclaim sports from those who are abusing them with their ego-and-greed-based actions.

But we have to overcome Sports Syndrome to do it.

That's what Howard Cosell called it.

It's a condition that describes people who are die-hard sports fans, athletes, coaches, administrators, and journalists at heart and who prefer the blind sanctification of sports to a comprehensive analysis of sports' impact—pro and con—on our culture. Those afflicted tend to resist virtually all sports-reform efforts. They too often look at sports through the starry eyes of their youth, when, from that perspective, all was well with the world of sports.

Unfortunately, there are too many Americans afflicted with Sports Syndrome today.

Those of us involved in sports, interested in sports, impacted by sports (that's basically all of us, isn't it?) need to stop looking at sports with such a romantic eye. We need to get rid of the taboo against being systematically critical of SportsWorld.

"It's tough because when it comes to sports, people basically want to be entertained," says sports journalist Robert Lipsyte. "They just want this pleasurable escape from reality. Sports are the most valid form of reality TV going. It's emotionally satisfying. It's wonderful entertainment. It's an easy way for members of dysfunctional families to talk to each other and express themselves.

"Throughout my career, perhaps the sentence I've heard most from people is, 'I turn to the sports pages because the news on the front page is too dreary.' Well, now the news in the sports pages is often dreary and most people don't like that. They want their sports entertainment left alone. It's that type of mind-set that makes what sports reformers are trying to do so difficult."

Too often, sports activists and reformers are seen as being too harsh. The thinking goes something like this, "Chill out, it's just sports, a harmless, fun, and entertaining respite from life issues that are more serious."

The fact is sport is a huge industry and a major sociocultural institution. It impacts our society in numerous, significant ways, across all demographic categories. As such, we must look at sports seriously and conscientiously examine today's sports systems and infrastructure so that we can work to enhance the positives and mitigate the negatives.

College sport is a perfect example of a topic needing a countrywide conversation.

"We need a reexamination of the role of sports in colleges," says Taylor Branch, author and American civil rights historian. "What are our priorities as a society? In some respects, sports have become more important than higher education. How much do we want sports to dominate what happens at our colleges and universities?"

Robert Davies, the founder and former chief executive of the International Business Leaders Forum, an organization dedicated to promoting global social responsibility, believed deeply in the power of sports to make a positive difference. He felt sport could help facilitate changes beyond the playing fields and locker rooms.

Before his death in 2007, Davies would regularly tell corporate leaders around the world that the visibility and popularity of sports, at both the local and global level, provided opportunities to improve health, develop communities, boost education and literacy, empower girls and women, and boost physical activity levels for disabled and low-income athletes.

"Sport is the most dynamic activity in the world today, with the potential to contribute powerfully to a better world," said Davies. "The power and influence of sport is only just being understood."

Davies felt we all had a responsibility to make that vision a reality. He was particularly tough on journalists. Davies once told an international conference of journalists and media representatives that "high-profile global sporting events are seen as a frontier for raising issues of injustice and social responsibility" and that the media have a responsibility to explore that frontier.

Unfortunately, a majority of today's sportswriters, broadcasters, and sports media executives continue to suffer from Sports Syndrome, and, thus, haven't heeded Davies' call.

It is the Sports Syndrome approach toward sports that is responsible for the sports department at newspapers and television networks traditionally being referred to as the "toy department." Interestingly, a lot of sportswriters describe their department this way as well. And as a result, they produce a lot of "journalistic pabulum," as sports sociologist George Sage describes their output.

But not all sports journalists are afflicted. Those who aren't provide a nice model for those who are.

Red Smith, perhaps the most famous sports columnist in American history, spent most of his career writing from a "toy department" mind-set. However, he completely changed his approach during the final years of his career. In the last interview he gave before his death in 1982, Smith had this to say about the responsibility of sports journalists:

My early feelings were that people went to sports events to have fun and that they picked up the sports section for the same reason. I thought it was my job to entertain. Often I just tried to do my soft-shoe dance and stay within the bounds of truth and propriety. For years I never spoke out against such controversial topics as the reserve system in baseball. I speak out more readily today and approach these topics with much more conviction than I ever did before. Listen, I believe that any sportswriter who thinks the world is no bigger than the outfield fence is not only a bad citizen of the world but also a lousy sportswriter, because he has no sense of proportion. He should be involved in the world in which he lives.

Evan Weiner is one of today's best sports journalists. He consistently produces high-quality interpretive and analytical journalism. He had this to say about the role of the sports media: "It's great to watch a game and report on it, but democracy deserves more than a box score when it comes to scrutinizing the business of sports."

While undoubtedly we have some quality sports journalists whose work extends beyond the "toy department" mentality, we still need a lot more muckraking sports journalists who are free of the Sports Syndrome affliction and who are willing to examine the sports systems and models at the foundation of today's sports issues.

The world of academia also deserves its share of criticism for the proliferation of Sports Syndrome. Our country's academics have, as a whole, chosen to view sports as frivolous and not worthy of in-depth scholarly inquiry. This is highly irresponsible, given the huge impact sports have on our culture—socially, culturally, and economically. One of the missions of our institutions of higher education is to provide leadership on important issues impacting society. For the most part, when it comes to sports, they're failing. And in most cases, it's the provosts and chief academic officers at our colleges and universities who brush off sport studies as unworthy.

However, one good example of academics taking a leadership role in this regard is University of California-Berkeley's course "Priorities under Pressure: A Critical Assessment of How the University's Core Mission is Affected by Intercollegiate Athletics." Generally, however, our institutions of higher education are dropping the ball when it comes to a serious examination of sport in society.

When it comes to sports, academia's focus appears to be on developing more commercial and entertainment sports managers and entrepreneurs through the growing number of sports management and marketing programs around the country. Sports ethics, and other important sports studies subjects, tend to get short shrift in these programs.

"Ethics has to be seriously dealt with in any sports management program," says Allen Sack, a sports management professor at the University of New Haven and formerly a sports sociology professor. "Sports management programs have the responsibility to not only develop skills and knowledge but also to engage in open dialogue on ethical issues. Ideally, there are courses in sports studies areas like ethics and sports policy in every sports management program."

Too many politicians are also afflicted with Sports Syndrome. As a result, they give the wealthy owners of professional sports franchises sweetheart stadium deals while allowing physical education and intramural sports programs to be slashed, as but one example of misplaced priorities. They also continue to allow professional sports leagues to operate as self-regulated monopolies. Politicians need to move away from being hero-worshipping spectator sports fans in their professional roles and toward promoting initiatives like more quality physical education and intramural sports programs in our schools.

Those in the fields of economics, law, and sociology must also take a portion of the blame for the lack of a sophisticated approach to sport policy analysis and development in this country.

Here's the stark reality: There is nothing comparable in the United States that impacts our way of life as much as sport does yet receives such a lack of serious analysis and inquiry. We have hundreds of public policy think tanks across the areas of politics, health care, economics, the military, energy, foreign policy, education, etc., yet only a few small entities that would be considered close to being sport policy think tanks in any meaningful way. That needs to change.

As a society, it is the thinking that sports are nothing more than fun and games and, thus, not worthy of serious analysis that has continued to haunt the development of an honest, in-depth exploration of modern sport and its social, cultural, economic, health, and legal ramifications.

Together we need to overcome Sports Syndrome and the general apathy that abounds when it comes to sports issues. We need to separate our love for the games themselves from our concern for the issues surrounding the games and how they impact all sports stakeholders. As demonstrated throughout this book, the world of sports is certainly much more than a diversion, much more than the "toy department" of life. It deserves the best of what journalists, academics, politicians, and the rest of us have to offer.

"There are so many people in this country who love sports but hate what sports have become," says Dave Zirin, one of our country's most passionate sports activists. "That's an opening for us to actually have an honest discussion about reclaiming sports from those who would use it to pump messages of militarism, racism, sexism, and corporate greed. We can go out there with a strong message that says we want to take our sports back, and we would be surprised at the audience we would find."

College professor Bruce Svare became a passionate sports reformer after becoming fed up with the sports abuses he saw on both the local and national levels. He ardently works to get others involved.

"By promoting reforms in countless community, state, regional, and national sports organizations, average citizens can be the instruments for change," says Svare. "All causes require this kind of grassroots effort, and sports reform is no different. The alternative—inaction and continued apathy—will only hasten the growth of a negative sports system that is devouring everything in its path."

THE NEED: CITIZENSHIP THROUGH SPORTS ACTIVISM

> More people are waking up and realizing that we need watchdogs in sports. We need more individuals and groups making us aware of what's going on. It helps make people courageous. I believe in preaching to the choir because you have to keep the choir brave. That leads to more individuals rising up. I encourage people to get started in their own communities. Really get out there. You might have to give up something, maybe boycott something, but take on the local sports bureaucrats. If we focus on sports reform at the lowest levels there will be positive ramifications all the way up to the pro level.
>
> Robert Lipsyte, activist sports journalist

While it's important to call on the sports media, academia, Congress, parent associations, and other groups to seriously look at the issues and problems in sports today, we can't count on these institutions and organizations to do this important work for us.

Thus, a big burden falls on the rest of us who have a stake in sports.

America needs more sports activists and reformers. Change agents, if you will. All significant social change begins not with government or corporations, but with citizens—we the people. And it begins at the grassroots level.

"Each person who cares about sports—through acts of moral courage—needs to work for small changes locally, in their schools and with their community sports organizations," says Lipsyte. "Everyone needs to think of all the small ways they can help protect our children in sports, and what they can do to make sports more pleasurable for young people, how they can increase positives like camaraderie and collaboration."

Political and business leaders didn't hand down the tremendous civil rights changes in this country. Rather, people pushed them up. Every day citizens stepped up, driven by courage and an intrinsic drive to act, to fight for what they passionately believed in, for what they saw as the right thing.

The same holds true for the sports activists and reformers throughout history who have made the world of sports better for us today. Those sports activists and reformers declared that the past and present weren't how things were going to be in the future.

You can be sure that many of the sports activists from the past, people like Jackie Robinson, Curt Flood, Billie Jean King—and others much less famous—were told by friends and relatives, "Don't bother, it's just the way things are." Thankfully, those fighters for justice from the past ignored those types of comments. They courageously moved forward and made a difference. Our country is a better place today because of them.

There are still brave sports activists fighting for justice in sports today. For example, despite working in an industry that is homophobic to a large degree, former Minnesota Vikings punter Chris Kluwe made his support for equal rights in marriage strongly and vociferously known as the 2012 NFL season was getting underway and as the November 2012 election approached.

About the same time, near the end of August 2012, Maryland state delegate Emmett C. Burns Jr. wrote a letter to Baltimore Ravens owner Steve Bisciotti, urging him to silence courageous linebacker Brendon Ayanbadejo's First Amendment rights. Ayanbadejo had been supporting the state's Civil Marriage Protection Act, the intent of which was to allow gay couples the ability to obtain a marriage license (Maryland voters approved the measure on November 6, 2012). Burns encouraged Bisciotti to "inhibit such expressions from your employee and that he be ordered to cease and desist such injurious actions." The public reaction against Burns's letter was so strong that Burns apologized for his actions a few days later. Everyday citizens rose up.

It's important to stress that a person doesn't have to be a professional athlete or have a lot of power, status, or money to make a difference locally or even nationally.

Rosa Parks's role as an activist is a well-worn example from the civil rights uprisings in the 1950s. But her actions and impact are still instructive: Do what you can, with what you have, where you're at, no matter your status in life. Parks, a seamstress at the time, was quoted as saying she was "tired of giving in" when asked what her motivations were for refusing to give up her seat on the bus to make room for a white passenger. Later, Congress called this struggling seamstress "the first lady of civil rights" and "the mother of the freedom movement."

It must be fully understood and accepted that those who currently have the power and money in sports aren't looking to change the sports systems and models in place. The vast majority of the wealthy and powerful in sports aren't interested in spending any time or money on the multitude of sociocultural issues and problems in sports, such as those outlined in this book. The current situation is working for these sports leaders; it has provided them with money and/or power. However, it has also resulted in a multitude of win-at-all-costs and profit-at-all-costs agendas that negatively impact the rest of us who have an ethical stake in sports.

So if we hope to overcome sports hegemony and the effects of Sports Syndrome in this society and take our sports back from the forces of WAAC and PAAC thinking, we must first understand the historical and sociological context in which sports have evolved to play the role they do in our culture today. How were the sport policies that shape our experience of sports today developed? And how are they maintained? What efforts resulted in positive change?

That is why I strongly recommended the two books I did in the introduction to this book: *A People's History of Sports in the United States* by Dave Zirin and *Sports in Society: Issues and Controversies* by Jay Coakley. They provide a great foundation for moving forward with your sports activism and reform efforts, at any level.

To ultimately succeed in this effort, we need to move ourselves and other potential sports reformers along the change continuum—from awareness of the issues and their seriousness, to understanding the issues, accepting the current situation, attitude change, and finally behavior change. We need sports reformers who are well-informed, passionate, and active. We need to create a sense of urgency.

As fans and participants, we have a passion for sports at their best. We need to convince our fellow sports stakeholders that sports can be better— for all of us. Sport can also be a great arena for challenging unjust practices in our society and creating social change that positively impacts our entire culture.

As Zirin says in *What's My Name, Fool? Sports and Resistance in the United States*: "We also have to realize that while these 'games' often provide a place where the dominant ideas of our society are reinforced, they can also be sites where those ideas are challenged or downright rejected."

The media will eventually help. This movement to change what sports can be will ultimately bubble up from the people—and then the mainstream sports media will be forced take notice and play a bigger role.

But first, as Zirin says, "Let's get the ideas out there in the oxygen."

An effective democracy requires active citizenship. It can take place in many areas. For sports lovers, what better way to make a difference in the world than through sports?

Basically, that's what I'm calling for in this book: citizenship through sports activism.

"Unless reform starts happening in a small way at the grassroots level with progressive, enlightened people, it's going to be difficult to accomplish," says Lipsyte. "Any revolution starts in the countryside, with the peasants rising up. The influence of the power holders in sports won't change unless the peasants rise up. . . .

"We need courageous individuals who are willing to take a stand with their local sports power brokers—the Little League directors, school sports administrators, etc. We need excited individuals to start reform in every state, to build state-by-state grassroots organizations. If we focus on sports reform at the lowest levels there will be positive ramifications all the way up to the pro level."

Sports reform is a challenging undertaking. It isn't easy. But it can be immensely fulfilling, especially when it becomes a collaborative effort.

For a good portion of his career, newspaper sports editor Lester Rodney was vilified from many angles for his columns attacking Major League Baseball for its color line. In fact, his efforts went underappreciated for decades. Finally, toward the end of his life, things turned around. He started to receive praise and recognition for his fight for social justice in baseball.

During an interview that took place when he was ninety-four years old, Rodney was asked what he thought about all the late-coming recognition.

"It's nice, but I don't make too much of it," said Rodney. "It just seemed like the right thing to do. We wanted to end the damn ban. . . . And when you changed baseball at the time, you changed the country."

We can look at those comments as Rodney giving each of us our marching orders.

As Martin Luther King Jr. said, "The ultimate measure of a man is not where he stands in moments of comfort and convenience, but where he stands at times of challenge and controversy."

In a 2011 commencement speech at Washington University, Elie Wiesel, a Holocaust survivor and Nobel Peace Prize winner, delivered a message with a similar theme.

"The greatest commandment in the Bible is 'Thou shall not stand idly by,'" said Wiesel. "Which means when you witness an injustice, don't stand idly by. When you hear of a person or a group being persecuted, do not stand idly by. When there is something wrong in the community around you—or far away—do not stand idly by."

Do not stand idly by. Summon a little courage. Get involved. Pick an issue. Do the right thing.

And help change the country for the better by improving the world of sports.

APPENDIX

Action Plan and Resources

CONSIDERATIONS FOR BUILDING AN ACTION PLAN

The person who has nothing for which he is willing to fight, nothing which is more important than his own personal safety, is a miserable creature.

John Stuart Mill

Idealism detached from action is just a dream. But idealism allied with pragmatism, with rolling up your sleeves and making the world bend a bit, is very exciting. It's very real. It's very strong.

Bono, U2 lead singer and philanthropist

Get started in your own community. Take on the local sports bureaucrats. Occupy Sports Street, at the local level, if you will.

Robert Lipsyte, activist sports journalist

When it comes to sports, we need to start thinking and acting as citizens, not just as fans and sports participants.

As Lipsyte suggests, we must think and act locally, as well as nationally. We must stand for justice at the local, state, and national levels. But we don't need to do it all at once. Any national reform measure will need the fuel of pressures from the grassroots level. For many budding sports activists and reformers, acting locally is likely the best first step.

To be an effective sports activist, reformer, or change agent (you pick the term you prefer) at the grassroots level, it's important to have an open mind regarding everything you know and currently believe about sports. It's time to take another look at sports from a justice and fairness perspective.

Sure, we can still take time to be sports fans and active sports participants. Sports are fun. But if we truly care about sports and what they might become for the next generation, we also need to take the time to be active sports citizens.

Our choice is simple and clear: Work to change things in sports in order to make them more fair, just, and ethical, or idly accept the serious—and growing—problems in sports that have largely come about due to win-at-all-costs and profit-at-all-costs thinking and actions.

Sports power brokers won't push for change in a sports system that gives them every advantage. Ultimately, however, as history has proven, moral power can overwhelm political and business power.

It's up to us.

A. Action Items

When it comes to sports citizenship, you can get involved as a generalist or specialist. Some sports activists and reformers pick a single issue to give their time, energy, and, in some cases, money to. That's fine. They are sports issue specialists. Others work for reform on multiple sports issues that they have a passion for. They are sports issue generalists.

While we all have certain sports issues that are more meaningful to us individually, it's important to remember that we are part of a larger movement, a sports-reform movement pushing for a more fair, just, and ethical world of sports overall.

What follows is a collection of ideas and potential action items to help start you on your citizenship-through-sports activism path. Along with the ideas in the "Recommendations" sections of the previous chapters, these items can help spur your individual or small-group game plans.

B. General Considerations

In the final analysis, changes in sport will be dictated by changes in our society, our needs, values, and perhaps outside influences. Perhaps you will be a catalyst for change in your community.

Ronald B. Woods, sports administrator and adjunct professor at the
University of Tampa and University of South Florida

- As a budding sports change agent there is one key question to consider when examining the policies, decisions, and actions of sports power brokers—whether those power brokers are running the NFL or the local Little League board: "Are they playing fair with—and considering the interests of—all stakeholders?" If the answer is "No" then it's time to get to work.
- Always look for the WAAC and PAAC mentalities that distort the true essence of sports. WAAC and PAAC policies are at the root of virtually all contemporary sports problems—at every level.
- Determine, and clarify, where you stand on important sports issues. Then send your views to the media, legislators, and relevant power brokers. Start a letter-to-the-editor campaign on a sports issue you're passionate about. Post your views on websites that are appropriate for your particular issue.
- In considering your positions on the sports issues important to you, look for civic engagement opportunities in your community.
- Take a few minutes to Google "tools for activists" and "tools for reformers." You'll find a wealth of good information for budding change agents, most of which is applicable for sports change agents. There is a plethora of ways to communicate and potentially unify people around good sports-reform ideas.
- Social media tools can help you find people who are like-minded in terms of today's sports issues and problems. Social media is also helpful in organizing and gathering momentum at the grassroots level.
- Join an established organization that's doing the work you're interested in on a particular sports issue. If there isn't an organized effort in your local area, consider starting one.
- Push your legislators to call for the creation of a national sports commission that can establish a national sports policy and code of ethics for sports, raise the profile of populist issues at a national level, and serve as an outlet and clearinghouse for concerns about contemporary sports issues. You could also explore the possibility of a sports commission for your state.
- Organize current and potential sports activists in your community through a local town hall meeting.

C. Pursue One or More of the Recommendations Outlined in This Book

This book contains analyses of a variety of important sports issues that deserve our full attention as a nation. Those issues include community ownership of professional sports teams; publicly financed stadiums and arenas; tyrannical coaches, especially at the high school and youth levels; cutbacks in physical education and intramural sports in public schools during a childhood obesity epidemic; overzealous adults in youth sports; equal opportunity in sports for all Americans; brain trauma and concussions in sports; the increasing commercialization and professionalization in college sports; sports and the media; and the need for a national sports commission.

Throughout this book there are lists of proposed recommendations for dealing with each of these issues. Some of the recommendations don't lend themselves to the work of individuals or small groups but others certainly do. If one of the recommendations strikes a chord with you, grab it and run with it.

Some people are solely interested in one particular area of the world of sports. Therefore, I've added some potential action items for specific levels of sports. Some of these are associated with earlier recommendations in this book, but others are added possibilities for those looking to make the world of sports better in their given area of interest.

1. Professional and Big-Time College Sports

As sports are not entertainment, neither are they business. Naturally, they are *in part* entertainment and *in part* business. When their essential spirit is corrupted by either the one or the other, the pain of loss is accompanied by disgust.

Michael Novak, author, philosopher, and theologian

- Create a "fans' council" and organize "accountability sessions" with a local professional sports organization and/or big-time college athletic department in your area. Make the media aware of your efforts. These accountability sessions can be used to make sure the power brokers are fully aware of and understand the concerns of fans and taxpayers.
- Push for legislation in your state that ensures that athletes injured while playing for universities and colleges have their medical expenses resulting from those injuries fully covered.
- Consider potential political and legal options against taxpayer-subsidized pro sports franchises and big-time college sports programs (operating under a government-sanctioned nonprofit umbrella). For example, you could attack the obscene scheme known as personal seat licenses (PSLs). Numerous pro sports franchises and big-time college sports programs require you to purchase a PSL in order to earn the *right* to purchase season tickets.
- Work to end the practice of building stadiums and arenas for wealthy owners financed by taxpayers, at a local or national level.

- Push your congressional legislators to remove antitrust protections for professional sports leagues in order to help limit the power of our country's pro sports cartels.

2. High School and Youth Sports

Those of us who really love sports are concerned that it be destroyed from being the experience it could be. . . . We want to save sports for what it can be.

Jack Scott, sports activist

- Resist the increasing commercialization, professionalization, and corporatization of sports at the high school and youth sports levels.
  - Corporations (e.g., McDonald's and Coca-Cola) are gradually taking over our high school sports programs through sponsorships.
  - At the youth level, many club sports organizations—with their strong economic interests—have increasingly usurped community youth sports programs, often limiting opportunities in the process.
  - Sport at its core—youth and high school—should be as free from profit-at-all-cost interests as possible. Fight back against creeping commercialization and professionalization in youth sports!
- Push for "fairness in sports" legislation at the high school and youth levels, e.g., call for increased budgets for physical education and intramural sports opportunities for all students, not just elite athletes. This is especially critical in this era of childhood obesity.
- Work for more safety measures in high school and youth sports, in particular in the areas of performance-enhancing drugs and concussions.
- Demand coaching education programs for all high school and youth sports organizations. These programs would address multiple issues, including eliminating the dehumanizing coaching tactics and behaviors too often prevalent in youth and high school sports.

3. State and Community Level

- Develop initiatives to increase *participatory* sports opportunities—at all age levels—in your community. *Spectator* sports are increasingly dominating our experience of sports. This has been detrimental in many areas, including negatively impacting our physical, mental, psychological, and spiritual health. Studies have shown spectator sports fans to be less healthy than nonfans. There needs to be a greater push to get all Americans, at all ages, active in sports beyond the spectator level.

- Create a statewide sports-reform network comprised of activist-minded sports stakeholders. This network could be designed to develop, advance, and publicize various sports policies and to promote legislation in areas such as concussion prevention and physical education in public schools, as but two examples.

RESOURCES: SPORTS-BASED REFORM ORGANIZATIONS AND TOOLS

Sport, Social Change, and Development

- **Sports Doing Good** www.sportsdoinggood.com Sports Doing Good's mission is to help inspire people to use sports as a tool for positive social change and to highlight the good work already being done by those in and around sports.
- **Center for the Study of Sport in Society** www.northeastern.edu/sportinsociety Based at Northeastern University, the center is focused on using the power and appeal of sport to create positive social change.
- **Journal of Sport and Social Issues** http://jss.sagepub.com The official journal of Northeastern University's Center for the Study of Sport in Society.
- **Beyond Sport** www.beyondsport.org Beyond Sport is a global organization whose mission is to promote, develop, and support the use of sport to create positive social change across the world.
- **Sports and Social Change** www.sportsandsocialchange.org This group's mission is to provide access to information, resources, and opportunities for those seeking connections with social change and cause-related organizations in the global sports community.
- **Sport and Development** www.sportanddev.org/en/toolkit Excellent source for information and tools in the area of utilizing sport for development, humanitarian work, and positive social change.
- **Change** www.change.org/Petitions A petition platform that anyone can use to start a petition to address sociocultural issues, including sport policy issues, at the local or national level.

College Sports

- **The Drake Group** www.thedrakegroup.org An advocacy organization dedicated to fighting for academic integrity in college sports.

- **National College Players Association** www.ncpanow.org The NCPA is a nonprofit advocacy organization that serves as an independent voice for college athletes looking to reform college sports and change NCAA rules.

Coaching

- **Positive Coaching Alliance** www.positivecoach.org PCA is a national nonprofit working to provide all youth and high school athletes a positive, character-building youth sports experience.
- **American Sport Education Program** www.asep.com Coaching education program built around the philosophy "athletes first, winning second."

Concussions and Brain Trauma

- **Sports Legacy Institute** www.sportslegacy.org The mission of the Sports Legacy Institute is to advance the study, treatment, and prevention of the effects of brain trauma in athletes and other at-risk groups.
- **CDC, Injury Prevention and Control: Traumatic Brain Injury** www.cdc.gov/concussion/sports/index.html CDC's research and programs work to prevent traumatic brain injury and help people better recognize, respond, and recover if a traumatic brain injury occurs.

Youth Sports

- **American Sport Education Program** www.asep.com Coaching education program built around the philosophy "athletes first, winning second." Excellent programs in the youth sports area.
- **Project Play** www.aspenprojectplay.org Project Play is a youth sports initiative of the Aspen Institute's Sport and Society program. The theme of the program is "Sport for All, Play for Life." The goal is to provide a platform for youth sports development in the United States.
- **Positive Coaching Alliance** www.positivecoach.org PCA is a national nonprofit working to provide all youth and high school athletes a positive, character-building youth sports experience.
- **National Alliance for Youth Sports** www.nays.org A youth sports advocacy organization focused on safety and positive instruction in children's sports.

Physical Education

- **PE4life** www.pe4life.org An advocacy and development organization for quality, fitness-based physical education programs in schools, K–12.

Girls and Women in Sports

- **Women's Sports Foundation** www.womenssportsfoundation.org Premier women's sports organization focused on improving the lives of girls and women through sports and physical activity.

Disabled Athletes

- **Disabled Sports USA** www.disabledsportsusa.org Provides national leadership and adaptive opportunities for individuals with disabilities.
- **Inclusive Fitness Coalition** http://incfit.org The IFC works to increase inclusion and access to health and physical activity for people with disabilities.

Sports Ethics and Character Development

- **Josephson Institute, Center for Sports Ethics** http://josephson-institute.org/sports Center focuses on utilizing sports to help build character while "pursuing victory with honor."

Sports Media

- **The John Curley Center for Sports Journalism** http://comm.psu.edu/research/centers/john-curley-center-for-sports-journalism Center explores issues and trends in sports journalism through instruction, outreach, programming, and research.
- **The Poynter Institute** http://www.poynter.org Poynter is dedicated to working toward responsible journalism in our democracy. The Poynter Review Project provided independent examination of ESPN content.

INDEX

UNIVERSITY OF ...
LIBRARY

ABOUT THE AUTHOR

Dr. Ken Reed is sports policy director for League of Fans. He is a long-time sports industry consultant, sports studies professor, sports issues analyst, columnist, and author.

Reed was a sports marketing consultant earlier in his career before switching career directions and utilizing his marketing and communications skills in a social-marketing role for a variety of sports, fitness, and education causes. He has delivered numerous professional-development seminars and presentations to sports administrators, educators, and business leaders.

Reed has long been a strong advocate for quality physical education and sports programs for all students, not just elite athletes. He created the Center for the Advancement of Physical Education (CAPE) for PE4life, a nonprofit organization dedicated to making quality daily physical education available to all students, K–12. He regularly speaks about how physical education, sports, and other forms of physical activity can improve academic performance, decrease behavioral problems, and enhance student wellness.

Reed has served as an adjunct faculty member for several institutions and has taught a variety of sports studies courses, including contemporary sports issues, history of sports, and sports sociology, along with various sports management courses.

Reed also has served as an executive board member and faculty fellow for the National Institute for Sports Reform, as well as on the board of directors for Positive Coaching, a nonprofit whose mission is to promote positive attitudes and behaviors in youth sports. In addition, Reed has served as an advisory board member for Metropolitan State University of Denver's Sports Industry Operations program.

He is the author of *Game Changer*, the inspiring story of Phil Lawler and his quest to make quality physical education a mainstay of our education system. Reed also has published a sports novel targeting young readers, ten to fourteen years old, called *Sara's Big Challenge*. The book's overarching theme is the importance of being true to yourself. In addition, he is a longtime sports issues columnist and feature writer for *Mile High Sports* magazine. His freelance columns and articles have appeared in numerous publications. He won first place in the 2005 Denver Newspaper Guild Awards competition for his sports commentary and was the recipient of the 2011 COAHPERD (Colorado Association for Health, Physical Education, Recreation, and Dance) Sportsmanship Award for his work on fairness and ethics in sports and physical education.

Reed holds a bachelor's degree from the University of Denver, a master's degree from Colorado State University (concentration in athletic administration), and a doctorate in sport administration (emphasis, sport policy) from the University of Northern Colorado. Reed lettered in baseball and basketball at the University of Denver and has worn many hats in the world of sports, including coach, referee, scout, manager, and sports talk-show host.

ABOUT LEAGUE OF FANS

League of Fans is a sports reform project committed to fighting for a level playing field in sports by enhancing the ability of sports fans, athletes, and other sports stakeholders to influence sports policy in this country. In effect, League of Fans serves as a sports-policy think tank.

League of Fans has a fourfold purpose:

1. To build momentum toward a vision in which all sports stakeholders are treated justly, fairly, and ethically.
2. To ensure that all those who have a stake in sports—including the millions of fans, sports consumers, sports participants, and taxpayers across the nation—have a voice in how sports are operated in this country.
3. To encourage sports stakeholders to become sports activists and reformers and to take action to improve the world of sports, wherever they're at, in whatever way they can, in an effort to help sports serve the public interest.
4. To increase the number of sports participants, at all ages, in the United States, because of sport's numerous physical, mental, emotional, and social benefits.

Please contact League of Fans with your thoughts, concerns, and ideas regarding any current sports issue or problem. One of the objectives of

League of Fans is to serve as a clearinghouse for all sports stakeholders on contemporary sports issues.

League of Fans
P.O. Box 19367
Washington, DC 20036
info@leagueoffans.org